P9-CKY-299

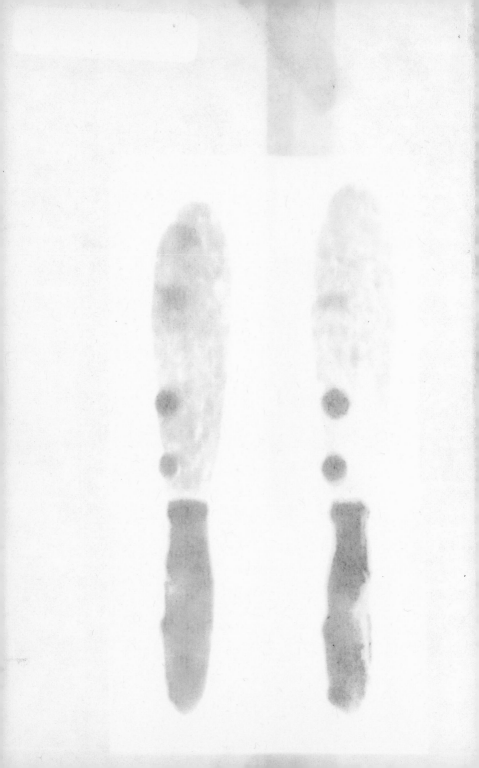

How We Play the Game

HOW WE PLAY THE GAME

Why Sports Dominate American Life

Richard Lipsky

BEACON PRESS

Boston

Copyright © 1981 by Richard Lipsky
Beacon Press books are published under the auspices
of the Unitarian Universalist Association
Published simultaneously in Canada by
Fitzhenry & Whiteside Limited, Toronto
All rights reserved
Printed in the United States of America
(hardcover) 9 8 7 6 5 4 3 2 1

Library of Congress Cataloging in Publication Data

Lipsky, Richard, 1947–
    How we play the game.

    Bibliography: p.
    Includes index.
    1. Sports and state—United States. 2. Sports—
Social aspects—United States. I. Title.—
GV583.L55   796'.0973   80-66074
ISBN 0–8070–3224–7

To David and Ruth, in the spirit of the agon, and for
Dorothy, for seeing so clearly and loving so well

Preface

IN THE TRADITION OF the Sportsworld I need to pay homage to those who made this book more than just a personal victory. The sports pages and magazines are filled with the tremendous sacrifices that make athletic triumph possible. We read of how the athlete often lost his or her will to continue until one instrumental person—a coach or a parent—interceded to bolster the athlete's failing courage. In the same spirit I need to acknowledge the support of Marshal Berman, my coach and friend. It was he who saw the possibilities in both me and the subject. It was he who read all parts of the manuscript with the kind of loving criticism that all books deserve.

I have also had the privilege of knowing and relying on the insights of a group of extraordinary scholars, including Mike Harrington, Murray Edelman, Ira Katznelson, Stuart Ewen, Allen Guttman, Ann Marie Walsh, Mike Krasner, Arthur Johnson, Bert Zweibach, Irving Markovitz, Yung Kum Kim, Marty Miller, and Rolf Myersohn. In addition, my chairman at Queens College, Henry Morton, whose book *Soviet Sport* showed the way, was an invaluable source of support as well as of ideas. I would also like to thank my editors, Tom Walter and Jeff Smith, who showed faith in the manuscript and edited it with a sensitivity that demonstrated an affection for the work as well as a keen understanding of its importance. I would further like to thank Sylvia Hecht, Norma Sileo, Edith Hatten, Louise Gikow, and Marsha Kaplan for their time and effort in the typing of various stages of the manuscript.

Outside the academic world, former sports reporter Robert Lipsyte, a man of extraordinary literary skill, was a model for me. He exemplified the possibility of combining intelligence, writing talent, and sports into a meaningful whole. His prose was always inspiring.

Finally, in the late innings of the project, I was fortunate to meet Dorothy Lipsky, whose tough but loving criticism helped see things through to the conclusion. She exemplifies the sports maxim "It's not who starts the game, but who's playing at the finish that counts."

Richard Lipsky
New York
April 1980

Contents

Illustrations

The euphoria of victory: John Havlicek, Red Auerbach, and Bill Russell in the Boston Celtics locker room (*Wide World Photos*)

Basketball ballet: Brian Doyle and Willie Randolph complete a double play for the New York Yankees (*Wide World Photos*)

Sports madness: "Wild Bill" Hagy and the Baltimore Orioles (*Wide World Photos*)

Aiming for the sky: Children in sports (*New York Post* photograph by Louis Liotta © 1981, *New York Post* Corporation)

The doctor operates: Julius Erving of the New York Nets flys in his Converse All-Stars (*New York Post* photograph by William Jacobellis © 1981, *New York Post* Corporation)

Playing the game: Richard Nixon in the Washington Senators locker room (*Wide World Photos*)

God Bless America: Jim Craig and Old Glory in their glory (*Wide World Photos*)

How We Play the Game

1. "Play Ball": How Sports Dominate American Life

"As civilization advances, the sense of wonder declines. Such decline is an alarming symptom of our state of mind. Mankind will not perish for want of information; but only for want of appreciation."

The Wisdom of Heschel

"Why did football bring me so to life? I can't say precisely . . . Whatever it was, I gave myself up to the Giants utterly. The recompense I gained was the feeling of being alive."

Frederick Exley

"In a symbol . . . there is concealment and yet revelation."

Thomas Carlyle

I HAVE BEEN involved with sports all my life as a player, reporter, and fan. I began as a devout disciple of the great Yankee teams of the 1950s. To me the two sweetest phrases in the English language were "How about that!" and "Going, Going, Gone!," uttered by the unforgettable voice of Mel Allen announcing the Yankee games. And I still vividly recall the day I *almost* caught Gil McDougald's foul line drive at Yankee Stadium.

When not actually watching or listening to the ball game, I was reading about my team and its heroes in the seven newspapers that my father, a theatrical press agent, would bring home every night. In the afternoons, after school, my friends and I would play punchball or stickball as we imagined that we too were, or were going to be, major-league stars. At school, especially in the afternoons, my thoughts would often turn to the upcoming Yankee game or to the anticipated pleasure of punchball until dark. At night I would toss my "Spaldeen" ball against my closet door as I enacted fantasy encounters between my Yankees and the hated Brooklyn Dodgers.

As a young adolescent I was captured by basketball. Why I switched allegiances is still not clear to me, but gradually my baseball devotion gave way to an intense involvement with "the city game." I played for my junior high school and high school teams, in outside leagues, and in the parks, playgrounds, and gyms throughout the city. During the winter, at least six nights of the week were spent playing the game. I would often practice with the high school team, come home and eat quickly, and be off to whatever gym was open that night. Basketball was booming on all levels in New York during this time. I followed the high school exploits of the legendary Connie Hawkins and rooted madly for the NYU teams of "Satch" Sanders, Cal Ramsey, Barry Kramer, and "Happy" Hairston. And then there was the New York Knickerbockers.

My father worked in the Herald Tribune Building in New York City and was friendly with basketball writer Irving Marsh. Because of this glorious connection, I was able to sit in seat F-4, right behind the Knickerbockers' bench. There I would listen to the squeaky voice of Ray Felix exhort his team and denounce the opposition. I would watch Kenny Sears hit that beautiful jump shot from the corner, leap to my feet as Richie Guerin drove the lane for his patented underhand "scoop" lay-up, and feel incredibly powerful as Harry "The Horse" Gallatan muscled in for a rebound. But, more often than not, my few moments of euphoria would give way to the premonition of disaster. Knick skillfulness would suddenly evaporate as the magnificent team of marauding Celtics from Boston, led by the satanic presence of Bill Russell, would sneeringly sweep past the Knicks' token resistance. If it wasn't Russell and the Celtics, it was the methodical brilliance of an Oscar Robertson–led team or the "show-time" virtuosity of Elgin Baylor and his Lakers. As if that weren't enough, a

3

Knicks' fan could look forward to Wilt Chamberlain single-handedly devouring the entire Knick team, as he did on the night in Hershey, Pennsylvania, when he scored 100 points against them. By being first a Yankee fan and then a Knicks fan, I understood early the potential range of the sports drama: from victimage and tragedy to redemption and triumph.

Despite, or rather because of, my involvement and expertise, writing a book on sports has not been an easy task. Sports always has been my refuge from what has often been a harsh and difficult reality. My real world was perplexing and painful, yet theoretically within the grasp of intellectual understanding. Intellectualizing and abstract introspection became a convenient pattern for denying the depth of the childhood hurts. The escape into sports provided me with a place to let go, a place of clear understanding and undeniable feelings. Putting this sacrosanct and personal area under a lens has caused considerable discomfort.

My resistance comes from another source as well. My involvement in sports was never really encouraged, and more often actively disapproved of. My mother harshly criticized the "grating" voice of my beloved Mel Allen and consistently told me to "stop bouncing that damn ball." Neither she nor my father ever came to a basketball game I played in. Through indifference and disapproval I learned to feel guilty about my own intense devotion. I realized other kids were devoted, but somehow I was different—more monomaniacal perhaps. The more I felt this difference the more involved I became. This legacy of guilt prevented my perceiving—right off the bat—that my own idiosyncrasy was connected to a whole world of equally idiosyncratic communicants.

The more I thought about studying sports, the more I realized how my own personal attachments were, in one sense, just the tip of an iceberg of intensity. Involvement with sports-playing and watching, reading, and talking dominates people's everyday lives. The "Holy Trinity" of baseball, basketball, and football is nurtured on the fields of rural America, the streets of urban ghettos, and the manicured play areas of suburbia. From its local and personal beginnings, the world of sports becomes a major form of national and social communication. Interest in and knowledge of sports make Americans of every region and class "available" to one another. Sports is the "magic elixir" that feeds personal identity while it nourishes the bonds of communal solidarity. Its myths transform children into their adult heroes while allowing adults to once again be children. All this rich excitement is part of a dramatic and symbolic world with important political as well as social ramifications.

The Sportsworld penetrates the core of individual identity. It is intensely personal yet shared through community rituals and the heat of sports conversations. Despite this obvious depth and breadth of involvement, the attempt to study sports has met with much resistance. This resistance is, in some ways, analogous to my own initial hesitation to study sports, but other factors are important as well.

The attempt to develop a political theory of American sports faces many obstacles. Sports and politics in America have traditionally been regarded as separate institutions. The gatekeepers of the Sportsworld itself have encouraged the belief that sports are "fun and games" and have vigorously fought any attempt at "outside" regulations. The separation of sports from the rest of society received judicial sanction in 1922 when the Supreme Court ruled that baseball was not a business engaged in interstate commerce and therefore was not subject to national judicial sanctions.

The separation of sports and politics has had ethical overtones as well. Sports, in contrast to politics, has been seen as a moral realm where character is built and virtue is pursued. The traditional lionizing of the sports hero clashes

5

with the negative public perception of politicians. This difference is the source of the fierce vigilance the Sportsworld's gatekeepers exhibit over the slightest appearance of corruption. An inability to police their own realm would lead, it is feared, to political interference that would destroy the moral and jurisdictional autonomy of sports. Robert Lipsyte captures the sports-politics separation:

All their lives they have been told that politics was dirty; that baseball was beautiful; that politicians were connivers; that ballplayers had the hearts of children; that [the] smoke-filled caucus room was the hellish furnace of democracy and that a sunny ballpark was its shrine and reward.

The difficulty of analyzing sports is increased by a pervasive "folk understanding" of American sports that has generated numerous self-proclaimed seers and journalistic experts. An interesting and nonobvious point often will bring a "Well, sure, everyone knows that" response from the involved fan. It only becomes obvious, however, after it gets articulated. Tackling such a subject is risky because everyone feels like an expert and a major insight is as valued as a two-day-old box score.

This popular folk belief—what I call the "I played second base in high school syndrome"—is abetted by academic hostility toward sports. On many college campuses the football or basketball team carries more prestige than any academic subject or academician. Historically, coaches and physical educators have struggled with professors and deans over the alleged overemphasis of intercollegiate sports. Additionally, coaches often are anti-intellectual, which strikes a responsive chord in the American public. Not to be outdone, intellectuals have exhibited an equally potent snobbery and disdain. As a result, the study of sports has been left to physical educators, who have not examined its larger political and social implications.

6

The creation of this sports (trivial) and politics (serious) dichotomy has been one of the most persistent obstacles to the serious examination of American sports. It is one thing to study societies with ministries of physical culture whose aims unblushingly reflect those of the ruling political party. It is quite a different task to analyze sports in a society where political and ideological purpose is often disguised and where socialization frequently is accomplished "through the back door."

Sports' location "above" politics was severely challenged during the upheavals of the 1960s. Each protest movement had its own sports section. The New Left criticized the "fascist," "anti-life," and "dehumanizing" aspects of sports. Black militants became enraged at quota systems and racial stereotypes. Women, during the latter part of the decade, began challenging sexual discrimination and supermasculinity.

These critiques attacked the rose-colored view that sports were untainted by political purpose and were aimed at two of the Sportsworld's weaknesses. Initially, the attackers enthusiastically exposed the Sportsworld's hypocrisy. After uncovering weaknesses of the Sportsworld itself, the critical thrust went on to reveal how the Sportsworld promoted the purposes of the larger political and social system.

If sports' defenders pointed out the beauty and joy of play, critics charged that sports "perverts" play in a joyless spectacle. If sports was glorified as an arena of mobility and equality, critics dramatized the elitism, racism, and inequality of the Sportsworld. If the athlete was portrayed as a creative worker, a craftsman, then the critics exposed the dehumanization of the jock, the strapping of the athlete into a rigidly stereotyped role.

7

The critical onslaught was relentless and exhaustive. If the world of sports valued discipline and authority, the critics gleefully attacked the Vince Lombardis and Woody Hayeses as lifeless martinets who subordinated all human relationships to the all-consuming goal of winning. If athletes were portrayed in the media as innocents, and their relationships with one another as the ultimate in spiritual camaraderie, critics detailed the money-grubbing, the sexual hypocrisy, the general mean-spiritedness of the players, and the shallowness of a locker-room scene that promised intimacy but rarely delivered.

After taking on the Sportsworld itself, the critics further described how they felt sports served the established power structure of the larger political system. The critics energetically red-dogged the "above politics" notion of the Sportsworld. While its defenders saw sports as separate from everyday reality, the critics zeroed in on sports as an "opiate" or "emotional Disneyland."

A primary target of the critical anger was sports' screening people from accurately assessing the harmful realities of the political and economic systems. While defenders saw sports as providing for the therapeutic release of pent-up hostility and aggression, the critics revealed how so often this emotional release prevented the causes of aggression and hostility from ever being creatively tackled.

The critical offensive clearly caught the Sportsworld off-guard. But the radical attack soon provoked an equally emotional defense of sports as integral to the "American way of life." This counterattack helped illuminate how sports had been put to ideological uses in the past. Only when athletic elites and their journalistic allies defended previously unexamined Sportsworld premises could these premises be linked to the structures and norms of the larger society.

The attacks and counterattacks lifted sports out of its sacred and unexamined playground. Within the space of a few years, sports had become a significant social fact. Yet

8

confusion remained, stemming partly from the critical assault on sports itself.

The critics were harshly, unavoidably "realistic." Legends must be demystified—in coaches' jargon, "They put their uniforms on one leg at a time, just like we do"—so players are not blinded by the aura of an opponent's reputation. This belittling strategy contains danger, though. "Cutting them down to size" runs the risk of seriously underestimating the opponent's real strengths.

The critics lack sensitivity to sports itself. Detailing all the "perversions" of the Sportsworld does not explain the seductive allure that sports has for its millions of emotionally involved fans. The critical devaluation makes it almost impossible to understand how any sensible individual could be taken in by the Sportsworld's sleight of hand. In order to understand the Sportsworld we need to identify with the straining athletes and the cheering crowd. We must be alive to the real drama, rich symbolism, and emotional strength of sports before we can begin to see clearly its important links to the larger political and social system.

The Sportsworld creates an extremely meaningful world for those who inhabit its arenas. As Neal Offen has observed: "Sports is life to the *nth* degree. It is life in extremis: every season you are born and you die, every forty-eight minutes or nine innings, you win and you lose. Every play encompasses an eternity."

The Sportsworld is a lived world, like those of literature and the theater, that is highly charged with human meaning. As a dramatic and symbolic world the Sportsworld has its own plots, scenes, characters, and settings. The game itself is the ritual hub of the sports universe; the team provides social structure; sports language gives the world cohesion; fans play the game vicariously through the athletes. Underneath and penetrating all the dramatic appeals is the powerful symbolism of play. The success of the Sportsworld rests on its ability to build its symbolic structure on the memory of play, on the illusion of play, and, finally, on the fantasy of play.

The political and social importance of the Sportsworld rests on its rich symbolism and dramatic structure. The dramatic power of sports pulls people out of their everyday worlds. As in the theater, sports encourages the willing suspension of disbelief, which enables the plots and characterizations from the larger society to be inculcated "through the back door." In this way the Sportsworld enacts the dominant values of the larger society while cultivating fan appreciation at the same time. Because we are transported to a playful world "above politics," we unwittingly permit values to make an "end run" around our conscious defenses.

The Sportsworld not only has acted and continues to act "through the back door" as a socializer of dominant values. It creates its own reality, an apparent autonomy from the mundane aspects of "real" life. This is a second source of its larger political and social impact.

Life may be dull, frustrating, and insignificant, but the Sportsworld is a world of feeling where *values* are still adhered to. Neal Offen again dramatizes the point:

There is a theory quite prevalent among analysts . . . that sports is a microcosm of life. It isn't . . . Sports is a world speeded up and a world of absolutes. There is good and bad, black and white, right and wrong. It's not gray and tentative like the real world. It's hyperlife under glass.

This "hyperlife under glass" contrasts sharply with a world of widespread alienation, a world in which people long for close individual and communal ties to overcome the impersonality and coldness of American life. Sports acts as the "magic elixir" that nourishes; the rest of the world merely drains.

The Sportsworld becomes a cultic movement that compensates for the deficiencies of the world surrounding it. James

10

Reston captures how sports compensates for the world's deficiencies: "The world of sports has everything the world of politics lacks and *longs for*. They have more pageantry and even more dignity than most occasions in American life, more teamwork, more unity and more certainty at the end than most things." The Sportsworld exquisitely provides the aesthetic form and supposed ethical content that for many Americans contrasts with a political and social world lacking either drama or ideals.

The Sportsworld not only creates an ethical realm, it also creates a bond that unites individuals. The Sportsworld is a more "personal," more "concrete," and more "intense" world than the rest of society. This intensity enables sports to become a refuge. Lipsyte dramatizes this theme: "Sports is a sweaty Oz you'll never find in a geography book . . . an ultimate sanctuary, a university for the body, a community for the spirit, a place to hide that glows with that time of innocence when we believed that rules and boundaries were honored."

Sports provides a "utopia of escape" that refreshes the partisan crowds and allows them to return with renewed vigor to their places in the political and social system. Analogously, the Sportsworld generates a diffuse "rain or shine" attachment to the ongoing political system.

If sports does act as a utopia of escape, it may also forestall real projects of reconstruction. On an individual level, the Sportsworld provides for the "sweet closure of anxiety," but the possibilities for personal growth and political change—two closely related themes—are effectively stalled.

The analysis of the Sportsworld that follows proceeds sympathetically, yet critically, inside the boundaries of the world itself. It transcends naive theories that depict sports as a "mirror of American life" but also moves beyond the radical arguments that see sports purely as an escape—an "opiate of the people"—without seeing at the same time how sports also

11

acts as the "heart of a heartless world." We will learn how sports acts both as a mirror of American life and as an escape from the same world whose values it most certainly does mirror in many subtle ways.

In this book I plan to illustrate through sports something of the structural malaise of American politics and society. If sports engenders the "sweet closure of anxiety," this book seeks to locate the genuine sources of this anxiety as the first step toward overcoming them.

2. "And Then I Thought about the Game . . . ": The Political Importance of Sporting Events

"Why does a man who does not like to go out in the warm Spring rain to get a newspaper, sit for three hours in a ten degree below blizzard watching a football game?"

Neil Offen

"So if we are all poets, and if all poets are pious, we may expect to find great areas of piety, even at a ball game."

Kenneth Burke

HOW DO YOU EXPLAIN your own insanity? It was the 1969–1970 basketball season, and the long-dormant New York Knickerbockers were coming to life. The Knick games elicited a manic intensity that completely engulfed me. Everything came to an abrupt halt as game-time approached. I would nervously read the afternoon paper, nibbling at tidbits of information that would enhance my enjoyment of the game. Out came my own rubber ball. When the game heated up, I would leap from my seat in an imitative frenzy of dribbling and jumping, collaborating with my heroes on the television screen. Conversation with me at these times was futile.

As the season built toward a dramatic climax I could not contain my hysteria. At a party one Saturday evening, I rushed past the hostess and said, "Where's the TV?" I found the sacred object, wheeled it into the living room, turned down the sound (I was being considerate), and immersed myself in the play of the silent figures before me. The lively talk that warmed the rest of the room might as well have been taking place in Peoria.

14

The game is the ritual center of the entire sports drama where the values of the Sportsworld are enacted in the clash of teams and the confrontations betweeen heroes and villains.

The intensity of the game's dramatic force brings to life the plots and characteristics of the Sportsworld and maintains its existence as a social life-world. The game takes on increasing importance in the everyday life and social structure of the surrounding community. This intense concern is revealed in the following illustration:

... Last season a man was fatally shot for playing the jukebox while the Bronco game was on TV. Amid speculation that an impartial jury could not be found anywhere in the Rockies, one Bronco fan asked, "Why have a trial? That fellow committed suicide."

The game as a ritual drama functions politically in several ways. As a stage for the portrayal of the "sports creed," it acts as a socializer of dominant values. Secondly, in towns throughout America, the high school, college, and even Little League teams are the major engineers of political cohesion. Preparation for the game and discussions of the game dominate the town newspapers and the everyday communication of its people. The following example comes from Vicksburg, Michigan, but it is by no means an isolated case: "If the Bulldogs win it is a matter of general elation in the town. A loss produces community depression, as well as lots of post-mortems about coaching strategy and the lack of moral fiber in today's teenagers."

In addition, sports is no longer merely a local matter. College teams clash intersectionally while local high school squads more and more frequently defend the civic honor in far-off geographic regions. Local youngsters are recruited for universities throughout the United States, and small towns point with pride to their favorite sons who dot the rosters of the major league teams. These events give people a sense of belonging to the Sportsworld, a sense that is reinforced through the national media. We all are literally as well as figuratively "playing the same game."

Finally, the dramatic symbolism of the game works a psychological spell. So much of political cohesion and legitimacy is built on unconscious foundations. As my personal account indicates, the game generates intense emotional ties. The game's euphoria compensates for an everyday life that is routine, anxiety-provoking, and often devoid of real meaning. This channeling of distress into the sports arena is politically significant.

The game acts as the focal point; it contains its own imperatives that link team, athletes, fans, and community. The players go through arduous preparation and mind-bending pressure before crucial contests:

The locker room before the last game. 13,909 wild fans inside. 10,000 people storming the gates. Players staring off into space. Russell throwing up. LeRoux winding and rewinding tape. Heinsohn sneaking a smoke . . . Sam Jones retying a shoelace for the twenty-first time. Auerbach, deep pouches in his eyes, a ragged dirty cigar poking out of his mouth, chewing the dead lip of it.

The sportswriters describe the dramatic meaning of the impending confrontation and the fans, like their representatives on the field, go through their own ritual of preparation in order to cut through the building tension. Frederick Exley's semiautobiographical saga, *A Fan's Notes,* captures how the fan, the team, and the players identify with each other:

Finally I turned to the sports sections. Even then I did not begin reading about the Giants. I read about golf in Scotland, surf-boarding in Oahu, football as Harvard imagines it played, and deep sea fishing in Mexico. Only then did I turn to the Giants, having by then already torn from the *Times* and stuffed into my pocket Arthur Daley's column, which I always saved to read but a couple of minutes before the kickoff, the biggest caramel of them all. I read every word of these articles over and over again. Occasionally the opposing coach would jeer. He would say the Giants are lucky, or that they were a bunch of weary old men . . . certain that the statement would be pinned to the bulletin board of the Giants locker-room in an attempt to infuriate the team to unbelievable feats. I would attach the insult to my heart and, with it, sneer and gloat as Robustelli, Grier, Huff and Katcavage pitilessly stomped their opponents into the hard, dry turf of Dallas.

In examining the sports ritual, its inherent structure and drama, it is useful to see it as a bracketed world, a world apart. This enables us to see clearly the formal outlines of the Sportsworld and facilitates a later understanding of how this form operates within the larger political and social context of American society. The perception of sports as a separate reality also better enables us to understand how a fan becomes involved with the game. On a conscious level, the fan sees sports as separate. Entering the arena or turning on his television, he feels he is leaving "reality."

Once the fan has begun his journey, he resents the intrusion of such real-life concerns as politics and economics. The popular dichotomy of sports as somehow "above" politics originates in the emotional needs of the fan to distance himself from nagging, everyday concerns. This leads the average fan to resent any attempt by the athlete to use the game as a political forum. When Tommie Smith and John Carlos raised a clenched black-power fist on the victory podium in the 1968 Olympics, the condemnation was swift and nearly universal. People do not resent only political statements by radicals though. Art Buchwald dryly recounted:

The Republicans bought time on both NBC and CBS for a special political appeal by President Nixon to be aired between half-time of all pro football games in the country. It was a blunder of colossal proportions. The silent majority is willing to listen to anything the president has to say six days a week. But Sunday they set aside to watch football. They don't want to hear about the Vietnam War, the economy, law and order or violence in the streets . . . It takes a lot to get the silent majority angry. But this was too much. When you mess around with their football games on Sunday, you're hitting them where it hurts . . .

The arena or ball park where the game takes place plays an important part in the creation of the separate world of sports. Often these arenas or parks are shrines amid the surrounding squalor. Exley describes leaving the decay of the South Bronx and walking into Yankee Stadium:

Yankee Stadium can be a heart stopping, an awesomely imposing place, and never more so than on a temperate and brilliant afternoon in late November. The vivid reds and oranges, the plaids, the golds and green of autumn clothing flicker incessantly across the way where the stadium, rising as sheer as a cliff, is one quivering mass of color out of which there comes continually, like music from a monster kaleidoscope, the unending roar of the crowd . . . I am yet unable to imagine a young man coming for the first time out of those dugouts—I am incapable of imagining stepping out and craning my head upward at the roaring cliff of color, wondering whether it is all a dream . . .

This emphasis on scenes is important for an understanding of the aesthetic appeals of the game. Murray Edelman notes that "many artists have recognized that the expressive power of their works is dependent upon their creating a world set apart from the one in which the audience lives and breathes, so that the spectators may find it easier to engage themselves with the artistic symbols."

The "suspension of disbelief" that accompanies this artistic distancing not only allows the audience to "engage themselves with the artistic symbols" but also allows for the inculcation of political and social values through an aesthetic "statue of liberty" play.

The arena, stadium or ball field is a bounded area. We are transported into a finite province of meaning with its own distinctive space, sense of time, and rules of causality. The

18

ball park is a "sacred space," made sacred by the pious attitude of the fans who enter it. Phil Berger captures this sacred quality:

Fans, Knick fans especially, had inordinate passion for the contestants. The Garden crowd was both up and heated. No gallery in the NBA had a quicker reflex to the inevitable errors that referees committed . . . or greater vocal muscle. Enthusiasm for the Knicks obscured the last bars of the national anthem and lasted a full forty-eight minutes for the home club.

The arena is not rooted in everyday reality, and its separateness is instilled in childhood. Jay Neugeboren captures the essence of the special feeling children have for *their* park or "yard" in his fictional account of a tarnished ghetto hero: "What schoolyard? Every basketball player, be he the world's best or the world's worst, lives for his schoolyard. It's where he grows, it's where he lives out his youth, where he finds his glory. For us it was an Eden!" The games in the arenas and stadia are extensions of these early playground experiences and dramatically link childhood activities with later adult identifications.

The game takes place in an atmosphere of piety. In many ways the ballplayers themselves can be seen as priests who represent us in a liturgy (the game) that is part of a sacred tradition. This is an important point because many parallels can be drawn between religious order and social order. Both need to integrate the disparate actions of individuals within a shared vision.

The athletic contest is performed under pressure, and the tension is magnified when two evenly matched teams or opponents compete. A "crisis" situation results. This tension is fed by various promotional techniques that underscore the stakes involved. Paul Gallico dramatizes this in his discus-

19

sions of the promoter Tex Rickard and the staging of boxing's first million-dollar gate:

It came quite naturally when Rickard made prizefighting not only respectable, but universally interesting and dramatic. . . he was definitely the first prizefight promoter to recognize that the essential features of every dramatic conflict are a hero and a villain, black and white, good and evil. . .

In team competition the media generally focus on sources of hostility between the two contingents and magnify past and present slurs. The monetary and psychic rewards of victory are trumpeted by involved reporters and further stimulate the sweaty-palmed fan who anxiously carries his rolled-up afternoon newspaper into the arena.

The pregame pressure fuels and is relived by the vocal power of the crowd. This tightly packed mass creates an in-group effervescence that generates a communal solidarity. The forceful emotions of the crowd give reality to the *home-court* advantage. Bill Russell explains how the crowd and players emotionally feed one another:

The people yelled and the sound came at us like waves . . . Then it became frightening. More than a mere sports event. We were not just beating this team. We were destroying it. The people were screaming, they were yelling for blood. They were yelling for all their frustrations, all their pent up feelings about the world. . . And we were responding. . . Compelled, unable to stop. Meshing together all the years and running like a precise, perfect machine.

The power of the audience, the Greek Chorus, gives the contest its dramatic and social reality. The athlete is like an actor enmeshed in a performance, fueled by the collective approval of the crowd. Away from the crowd the athlete talks of "life on the run," the loneliness and nomadic existence of the road. He fears the end of his career because it will mean the termination of his crowd-induced high. The talk of the

20

loneliness of the road accentuates the warmth and communalism of the arena. "The hoo-rah that the fans gave the games' player animated his nights and conferred on his work a blessed immediacy that solitary artists never had. But the blood that was pumped up by the clamor...turned still in the aftermath..."

During the game, the social euphoria generates a festive communion and sense of solidarity between the players and fans. The tension-filled atmosphere is punctuated by chants of "Defense, defense," "We want a hit," "Let's go, Mets!" Simultaneous cheers, groans, sighs, and boos break down the walls of isolation. The spectacular slam-dunk generates a series of hand-slapping, fist-raising identifications. The atmosphere induces a "cultic piety" among fans. Orrin Klapp explains: "Spectators also help make cults by assuming the role of devoted fans...there is a point at which the admiring audience becomes a worshipping congregation."

The crisis situation is magnified by the sheer physical risks involved and by the violent intensity of the play. As Bill Russell points out, "But if it all sounds like fun, it's not. It is high speed applied psychiatry. It is a fight to the finish, a capsulized forty-eight minute version of a guerilla war or the struggles and hates and frustration and successes of a lifetime."

The baseball can kill, the cleat can lacerate, the forearms can maim. The player lies still on the field, the boxer quivers on the ring's canvas, the runner collapses in exhaustion at the finish line. The protective gear underscores the danger that awaits, while the bandages and braces highlight the misfortune of past combat.

This physical intensity is dramatized by George Plimpton's Walter Mitty adventures as a participant-observer. Plimpton sees firsthand—and shakes at the sight of—the athlete's awesome skills and sheer size: "...the old whack of football gear when the lines came together sounded like someone

21

shaking a sack of Venetian blinds. The spectators on the sidelines gave a gasp at the violence of the contact seen from as close as they were. Inside the helmet I felt my own jaw drop slightly and my eyes widen."

The physical excitement and danger of the game have their own inherent appeal and can even touch those who are not deeply immersed in the fortunes of the contestants. The game is, however, the dramatic enactment of a whole series of plots and subplots involving players, teams, and even owners. The game "makes flesh" an entire world that is supported by sagas in the popular magazines, controversies in the daily papers, and inside stories in "behind-the-scenes" biographies. Most serious fans maintain a persistent set of identifications not only with their own teams and heroes but with the entire structure of the Sportsworld. The game is an enactment and test of the "sports creed" at the same time that it reinforces the more parochial team loyalties.

As our representatives, the athletes sacrifice for "good" principles of social order. The athlete practices self-denial in the form of years of hard training. The training camp itself is often an all-male refuge (away from the "soft" allure of women and the clamor of domestic strife). The popular biographies of players also communicate self-denial and sacrifice. We learn (if we don't already know from our own early attempts at athletic success) how they struggle and the obstacles they overcome in order to reach the privileged pinnacle of their profession. The ideas of sacrifice and devotion are also upheld by the stories about failed athletes who are crestfallen after unsuccessful attempts to make the team (being cut from the team is described as having "died"). Their failure underscores the honor of those who play.

On the field our heroes are ready to do battle with the enemy. This warlike symbolism has often led critics to inveigh against sports' militarism. There is, however, a huge difference between symbolic murder and actual killing. More

22

to the point, I believe, is the ability of the game to instill a sense of dramatic purpose. Our players, in their pursuit of victory, will stake their reputation on the outcome of the contest and often will endure the pain of humiliation or injury. The injunction to "play with pain" highlights this principle of mortification. When an athlete does overcome an injury to lead his team to victory we are moved by his sacrifice.

A knee-braced Joe Namath, a broken-nosed Jerry West, a Bobby Orr with six knee operations exemplify the principles of sacrifice and mortification. The most intense enactment of these dramatistic principles occurred when a seriously injured Willis Reed led his team to a championship:

The Knicks took the floor without Reed. He stayed inside trying to pinpoint his pain for Dr. Parkes. Once it was localized the Doctor would give him a shot of cortisone, an anti-inflammatory agent, and a shot of Carbocaine, a pain-killer...The word was over the airwaves during the day that he would play. But as the crowd eyed the foyer...there was still no Reed. Then, minutes later, Reed was there. He looked straight ahead, his lips pursed. It had the melodrama of the cinema death walks...the crowd lit up. They cheered even his warm-up shots...in a series turned adrenal, New York had the trump in Reed.

Reed's example and the crowd's fever ignited the Knick team. If Willis could show up to play, anything was possible.

All the sacrifices point toward the central goal of victory. Victory defines success with a clarity seldom achieved in the real world. Teams and the individual athletes, as our representatives, hold our destiny in their hands. George Allen drives this point home: "One of the greatest things is to be in a locker room after a win...The rewards are not necessarily tangible. It's the hard work and the agony and the blood and the sweat and the tears. When you lose it's a morgue. That's

23

the way it should be because you've failed. . . The only way to get over a loss is to win the next week."

The players are aided in this struggle by the coaches or managers, who personify authority. The coach dramatically paces the sidelines (watch Jack Ramsay or Larry Brown) and intensely gestures at *his* players, visibly wincing at their glaring mistakes, patting fannies as a reward for excellence. The baseball manager (Leo Durocher or Billy Martin, for example) rushes out to upbraid an official who has been actively "persecuting" his team. Through the assumption of leadership the coach also becomes the focal point when the team falls apart and the players don't perform.

Winning or losing has been likened to life and death. It is perhaps more helpful to see winning and losing as aspects of redemption and victimage. By pursuing victory (through a process of identification with our heroes) we are attempting to avoid being victimized—humiliated. Winning redeems us and at the same time we are at one with the order of the Sportsworld—self-sacrifice, "character," mental toughness, teamwork, and discipline. In losing, the other team highlights our own successful enactment of the sacred values—just as order is defined by disorder, and righteousness by heresy. The jubilant, cheering, champagne-pouring victory celebration is punctuated by the head-in-hands, tear-stained losing locker room.

When the game begins to go poorly for our side, the search for scapegoats begins. The fans begin to get restless. They yell for the benching of their favorite whipping boy or heap abuse on the million-dollar slugger who strikes out. The coach tries new players (often the "wrong" ones as far as the experts in the stands are concerned). If the team continues to slide, the coach himself can become the focus of a huge reservoir of frustration and anger. When the losses begin to pile up, this can turn the stadium into a crucible of vindictiveness.

24

Harland Svare of the San Diego Chargers was one coach who found this out. Svare, portrayed in the press as lazy, soft, vicious, and unstable (the reporter often becomes as angry and frustrated as any fan), was the target of a "crescendo of anger":

The crowd was at full howl when we reappeared, like the big cat house at the zoo just before feeding time. The roar changed into one of approval when the Falcons streamed to the opposite bench!... The wildness and rage building in the sound of the crowd I had heard the likes of only in Oakland and in Baltimore. There it was always for the alien team. Here it was for the home team...

Arnold Mandell relates how Svare became the scapegoat for all the anger initially directed at the players and was forced to dodge bottles and other thrown objects. On his way out of the stadium—after another decisive loss—his car was set upon by a howling mob and he had to be rescued by city police.

The coach becomes the ritual victim whose "sacking" affirms the cohesiveness of the group and righteousness of its principles. The players, realizing their own role in the tragedy, yet glad to have someone else take the blame, band together with a new sense of purpose. The fans too, their anger released, are free to use their energies to again support the team.

The process of victimage and redemption is most visible in the reaction of fans to the opposing team or an especially hated opposing player. A few years back, Knick fans derisively chanted "Good-bye, Louie" as their team beat the Lew Alcindor–led Milwaukee Bucks. Wilt Chamberlain, as "Goliath," always served as the ready-made foil for ambitious basketball "Davids" and their followers. The ritual drama of the game first heightens, then reduces anxiety by externalizing anger and frustration, channeling them against a concrete and visible enemy. Bill Russell recollects this process:

We were running over them like a man might run over a floundering cripple. . . It was my worst moment in sports. There was the horror of destruction, not the joy of winning. The horror of knowing you are the instrument of the worries of man calling out: "Destroy . . . Kill . . . Ruin." The long road had come to a peaceful end. We knew—and did not know—we sensed, and did not completely comprehend, that we had taken sports out of the realm of a game.

The game provides an arena for heroism, a stage designed for drama. It provides the opportunity to visibly succeed or fail under situations of intense pressure. Free from the dullness and confusion of a world around him, the athlete is allowed to strive for greatness, encouraged to stand out among his peers. Newspapers publish accounts of the athlete's humble, often minority group origins and his "ordinary" private life. The ordinary-extraordinary dichotomy feeds the need of the average Clark Kent to toy vicariously with the possibility of becoming Superman. Paul Gallico exquisitely plays with this theme:

All the great legends of the ring are built upon the picture that the average man has of himself as he would like to be, a combination of D'Artagnan, Scaramouche, the Scarlet Pimpernel and Jack Dempsey. If we could, we would all be gentle, soft spoken creatures tender with women, cool and even tempered, but once aroused— "Whap!" A lightning-left to the jaw. Down goes the truck driver or hoodlum. We mentally dust our hands, readjust our cravat, smile pleasantly, step over the body of the prostrate victim and carry on.

Then there are those villains we love to hate. Wilt Chamberlain as Goliath; Cassius Clay as "uppity nigger"; Joe Namath as wise-guy braggart; Reggie Jackson as the spoiled superstar. On the other hand, the quality of the sports drama makes it possible for one person's hero to be another's villain. The possibilities here are truly protean. Like the heretics of old, these villains define through counterpoint the "good" principles our more favored ballplayers possess. The failure, vanquishing, or banishment of the villain is necessary in the social order of the Sportsworld—and beyond. As Hugh Duncan sharply points out, "In a time when we cannot grapple directly with our villains, it is a great relief to do symbolically what we cannot do in reality."

The game, of course, has its own set of rules, which are dramatically and personally enforced by the umpires and referees. The grandiloquent "Out!" or "Strike!" is a staple of the sports cartoonist. The dramatic rule enforcement also affirms our faith in the order of the Sportsworld. As former umpire Babe Parilli remarks, "...if a baseball umpire is to give the impression that he is sure of his judgment, he must forego the moment of thought which might make him unsure of his judgment; he must give an instantaneous decision so that the audience will be sure that he is sure of his judgment."

The rules create a legal drama, seen clearly in the institutional rhubarb, the coaching tantrum, and the inevitable ejection designed to uphold the sanctity of the legal-moral order. When the home team begins to struggle, however, the umpire easily becomes the scapegoat whose mistaken judgment "caused" the defeat. The fans' chance to vocally protest gives them the feeling of democratic participation. The protest, however, is purely symbolic and cathartic and is only directed toward the applications of the rules, rarely at the rules themselves. During the game it is clear to both players and fans that certain actions will lead to censuring—that a whole ethical-legal structure stands behind the man in the striped shirt or blue suit.

One more observation should be made. A perennial problem hanging like a shroud over the integrity of sports is the danger of a rigged contest. When the possibility of "fixing" arises, the Sportsworld unites behind a strong executive who purges victims to insure the "integrity of the game."

27

The questions of drug use and violence have invited similar executive responses in recent years.

The game as the hub of the sports drama links the fans not only to an ethical structure but to an entire historical tradition. The game is part of a season that itself connects with patterns of lifetime involvement. Archetypal Knick fan Sidney Asofsky had "been with" the Knicks through seasons of humiliation. The long-awaited success of his team brought with it a feeling of rebirth, a vivid sense of redemption:

When Mullaney made no changes at the start of the second half, a thirty-three year old Knickerbocker fan who history had taught circumspection nevertheless thought it in the bag. But, however keen a basketball dialectician Asofsky was, the years had trained his biology to fear and no amount of rational powers could change that. In the final twenty-four minutes of the game, Asofsky said yes, yes, it's happening and tried to relax. But when it was over and the Knicks were at last champions, 113-99, Stanley Asofsky had his underwear slipping and knotting against his legs . . . Yes, yes, yes, it had happened. The Knicks were the champs. At last.

Each game, each season for that matter, has a sense of destiny and meaning. The thrill of consummation animates each segment of the Sportsworld lifetime. In real life we only vaguely feel the future as a total experience that is coming because of our present acts. The game (and the season) gives the Sportsworld a dramatic wholeness—a sense of purpose that contrasts with the real world.

The game symbolizes life in the real world and plays an important role in the process of socialization. In the first place, the game is democratic. It is played by equals according to merit—symbolizing the principles of an open class structure. From its beginning as a mass phenomenon, sports has been a visible avenue for ethnic mobility. That the realities of successful mobility in real life differed from the sporting myth does not take away the game's symbolic resolution of the tension created by the gap between expectation and reality.

The game has also, since the inclusion of blacks in baseball in 1947, presented a dramatic stage for racial harmony: the black sprinter and the white sprinter running a victory lap arm in arm, the black halfback leaping for joy into the white tackle's arms, the white coach embracing his black superstar. The visual symbolism takes on mythic dimensions. Recently, to be sure, many critics have focused on incidents of racial tension, quota systems, and systematic exclusions of black and Hispanic players. The critics excellently deflate the overblown prose of team press releases and the sentimentality of certain sportswriters. Their critiques, however, do not detract from the exemplary nature of black-white relations in sports.

The sports team is a visual example of black-white cooperation. In addition, almost all the popular biographies of players and teams emphasize the "beyond racism" nature of sports. Clearly, the level of intimacy never reaches the heights that the rhetoric of the Sportsworld gatekeepers achieves. That does not take away from the symbolism, as John Wooden relates:

One of the most gratifying moments in my coaching career came afterwards in the Astrodome as I walked in our dressing room door. I heard some writer ask Curtis Rowe, "What kind of racial problems did you have on the UCLA team?" Curtis, without hesitation, looked at him in that firm strong way of his and said, "Coach Wooden doesn't see color."

The ferocity of the debunkers only underscores the power of the symbolism.

Inculcating "faith" in the rules is an essential component of socialization. The rules are the scenic backdrop for the competitive struggle: they induce the idea of equality of competitors, but the reality is different. People are induced to

29

"play the game" no matter how unrealistic their chances for success are.

The game is an affirmation of legal order, yet the Sportsworld's legal operations are out of the hands of players and spectators alike. Decisions are handed down like obiter dicta for "the good of the game." Investigative bodies operate above and beyond any safeguards of due process. Yet Sportsworld participants and fans acquiesce in rules that are handed down. This acquiescence, or "rain or shine attachment," is crucial to the stability of political systems. The game even offers the disgruntled a way to protest and "participate" by verbally assaulting officials.

The game is also a metaphor of social cooperation. As American society becomes more complex, the chances for individual mobility lessen dramatically. Competitive drive, meanwhile, must be leavened by a sense of "teamwork." People need to be induced to take part in the often oppressive intricacy of the division of labor. The team games, especially the more corporate ones of football and basketball, inculcate the ethics of cooperation. The late Milton Gross captures this symbolism in writing about the Knicks: "They seemed to be wired to the same circuit so that any one of the five on the floor reacts to what the other four are trying to do." Even the discussions of baseball, the most individualistic of team sports, emphasize the importance of cooperation and team morale.

Cooperation and competition, equality and mobility are antithetical themes in American life. The game dramatically synthesizes these ideals. It provides a visible symbolic resolution of the struggle between individual success and the cooperative ethics of the community. Everyone on the team strives to be a starter. Yet although we compete within the team, we are still a *team* (the idea of "antagonistic cooperation"). Bill Russell gives an example:

I was taking Risen's job and I would not have blamed him if he had

30

hated me. Instead, Arnie Risen went out of his way to help. I've never forgotten him for it and I never will. Remember this was professional sports and the money was on the line. Risen transcended the norm for a professional sportsman. He was a team man all the way.

The struggle between the two opposing teams affirms the larger rule-bounded structure and cohesiveness of the Sportsworld itself. When the game ends, the cutting comments that had marked the pregame atmosphere are no longer appropriate. The losers bravely congratulate their conquerors, who repeatedly reply, "You guys played a hell of a game. We were lucky to win." When the battle's heat subsides, winners and losers, fans and players, are all joined in their common allegiance to the contest and to the world it represents.

The game is the garden where the values of the larger society are grown through the "stylistic subterfuge" of creating a mythical and unproblematic world. Obstacles that symbolize the barriers of the larger political and social system are dramatically resolved.

The Sportsworld exists as a world with a transcendent meaning all its own. This transcendence is another source of its political impact. The "apartness" of the Sportsworld, its unique sense of purpose and drama enable it to exist in counterpoint to the larger bureaucratic world of machines and techniques. The Sportsworld thus bolsters the stability of individual lives and the political cohesion of the larger society.

The games and players of the Sportsworld create a meaningful, seasonal cycle, in sharp contrast to the routine of the real world. Gallico captures this essence:

They were queer fascinating folk who peopled this weird world and who became my temporary companions as the seasons brought

31

them around, each in turn, almost as though they were papier-mâché figures on a slowly revolving cyclorama. It seems, in turn, as though I never knew days, weeks, months... but only sports seasons... all coming round year after year regularly as if driven by clockwork, with their costumes and paraphernalia, their lingo, their camp followers, and their famous characters.

When life offers fewer opportunities for "emotional pay-offs," a vacuum of feeling is created that threatens the ongoing stability of society. The game feeds the emotions and provides a collective strength of purpose that is rarely seen in the real world except during wars and disasters.

Our era is distinguished by a widespread "collective search for identity" that shows up in the search for cults, heroes, popular movements, or religious sects that can anchor a frequently tenuous sense of self. These ad hoc movements provide a social structure and a value-centering that links disparate individuals through collectively affirmed feelings. The passionate desperation of this search emerges from the value confusion and massiveness of a scientific, bureaucratic, and impersonal technical world. In response to this world, our perspectives often become more skeptical and impious. Yet, without some central orientation, we flounder; anxiety swells in us and seeks a release.

Our society spawns numerous organizations that absorb our dues but not our devotion. Cults rise and then decline; we shop in the religious marketplace for a more relevant road to salvation. Disenchantment is inevitable. The existence of this value instability and emotional vacuum is fraught with danger. The ability of political sorcerers to stage massive community dramas attests to this. Kenneth Burke drives this home in his discussion of Nazi mass meetings and speeches:

And is it possible that an equally important feature of appeal was not so much in the repetitiveness *per se,* but in the fact that, by means of it, Hitler provided a "world view" for people who had

32

previously seen it piecemeal? Did not much of this lure derive once more, from the "bad" filling of a "good" need?

It is useful to see the Sportsworld as a symbolic mass movement with myths and rituals of its own. Here is a world that can engage us actively and vicariously from childhood to old age. Here is a world where one game can feel like a lifetime replete with numerous little deaths and rebirths. Through all the media it penetrates our everyday lives, forming a "national sports consciousness." It is a complete universe that warms the cold bars of our iron cage.

The Sportsworld is rich in symbolism and excitement. It also echoes the deficiencies of the larger environment within which it is absorbed. However, can we not press for more satisfying remedies for these deficiencies? We must remember that when we return to our private lives from an emotionally uplifting game somebody else is cheerfully counting the receipts.

3. "Wait Till Next Year":
The Political Implications of
Team Allegiance

"We learn from the Boston Celtics even while we enjoy them."

Jeff Greenfield

"The season was one of the great experiences for the city, for the team brought people from all walks of life together . . ."

Former Mayor Walter Washington
of the District of Columbia

"Whatever it was, I gave myself up to the Giants utterly. The recompense I gained was the feeling of being alive."

Frederick Exley

"It's easy to be a fan of a winning football team: it takes dedication and character to be an Iowa fan."

Letter to *Sports Illustrated*

THE LATE 1960s and early 1970s were an odd mixture of pain and delight. In order to avoid the rice paddies of Vietnam and Cambodia, I had signed up for a form of alternative combat in the public schools of New York's inner city, even though I was armed with a bare twelve credits of education courses. It was a constant battle to maintain my self-esteem.

After finishing a draining day in the classroom, I would rush to Hunter College to tackle Marx, Hegel, and Plato in pursuit of a doctorate in political science. Against this pressured background, a marriage with built-in weaknesses began to unravel.

In the midst of this threatening environment, I had a joyful sanctuary of frenzied calm. I entered the world of the New York Knickerbockers and found an island of safety. With Willis and Clyde, Tricky Dick and Dollar Bill, I found the warmth and acceptance of Home. I was able to leave behind

35

the painful realities of work and home life and find solace and fellowship in the Knickerbocker community.

The allure of the Knicks was intensified by their gradual transformation from humiliated bumblers to haughty champions. The possibilities of rebirth and revival were dramatically brought home to me through fast breaks and full-court presses on the Madison Square Garden stage. The long era of our humiliation had ended.

I had adjusted to the atrocious play of the Knicks in somewhat the same fashion as the downtrodden rationalize the inevitability of oppression. Year after year of false messiahs had dulled my expectations, but hope—albeit tinted with skepticism and resignation—had always remained. Slowly, this mixture of hope and skepticism was transformed in the electric excitement of an eighteen-game winning streak, playbook perfect team play, and heart-stopping comebacks. My season ticket gave me entry into a Madison Square Garden revival meeting. The primitive emotional upsurge of the Garden crowd did not come from the chic newcomer-fans. It came from the lost tribe of Knick faithfuls, who had personally suffered through the desert years.

As the Garden became a place of worship, the sports pages of the New York *Post* became holy writ. Milton Gross, Lenny Lewin, and Larry Merchant caught and fueled the devotional spirit. Fans read about the dramatic confrontation before entering that night's contest. The next afternoon, we would check our own expertise and interpretations against the *Post*'s. A sense of community grew in the heat of Knick artistry. I remember leaping out of my seat at a Willis Reed slam-dunk and running down the aisle getting "five" from a congregation of communicants. A warm camaraderie built as the Knicks began to redeem us from our years of suffering.

The road to redemption led to a climactic seven-game play-off series with the Los Angeles Lakers. During the play-offs, almost everything took a back seat to the Knicks. All thoughts were directed to the upcoming games, and the streets and stores were alive with highly charged and expert talk of Knick strategies and possibilities. I remember Passover that year. During the Passover service, the front door is symbolically opened for the entry of the prophet Elijah. I slyly offered my services as door-opener and disappeared for twenty minutes of crucial fourth-quarter action (while learning the difficulties of dual religious affiliation).

The stage was set for dramatic confrontation. In game five, Willis Reed had fallen with a serious leg injury. Without Reed, the Knicks had been crushed by the Lakers' Wilt Chamberlain in game six. The reports on the morning of the seventh game said that Reed would play, but no one knew how well or how long. I took off from work that day, and the nervous tension became simply unbearable as game-time approached. My hands and feet were ice cold, and the knot in my stomach grew larger and larger.

The warm-ups began without Willis on the court. No one really watched the Knicks shoot around; all eyes were on the players' entryway. And once Reed's mountainous figure graced the entry a crescendo of noise arose. The feeling was a mixture of relief and triumph. It was the same feeling I used to get as a kid when the cavalry appeared on the hill to rescue the helpless settlers. Yet this was different. I was at one here with the helpless settlers like never before. All the years of playing, fantasizing, and identifying were telescoped in that dramatic instance. My own faith and courage returned, pinned on the limping figure of Captain Willis Reed.

Fans and players were locked in a communal embrace. An intense Bill Bradley became even more determined as his shooting tempo increased. All the players' shots seemed to embody the air of confidence that was permeating the building. The faces on the Lakers told the story. When Reed had appeared, they all stopped their warm-ups and simply stared at him. They seemed to understand with resigned

37

inevitability that the unfolding plot made their own intervention fruitless. Reed dramatically hit his first two shots, and the whole Knick team (who could forget Dave Stallworth's incredible underhand reverse lay-up?) punished the Lakers in a setting that combined celebration with the righteousness of religious retribution.

That moment was the emotional peak of my life. I was soaking wet. I yelled out the window. My suffering had been redeemed. I felt as if no one could ever understand my feelings at that moment. Amidst the screaming of thousands, I felt as if I had special feelings that no one else could share. Ever since I had been a 5′1″ seventh-grader, I had dreamed of being a Knick. I had practiced for hours, six and seven days a week. I was a good player. I played in high school, I played in college; but I was never going to be a Knick. Yet somehow at that moment I *was* a Knick. I had given the team and the game of basketball a huge chunk of my emotional life, and I was repaid in this moment of mystical communion.

Many observers of the American sports scene, as well as numerous social thinkers, have been quick to point out how sports teams help produce political and social integration. The team plays an important part in reinforcing community cohesion on all levels of American society. The belief in the powers of team symbolism is so strong that many sociologists and industrial psychologists either recommend creating "team spirit" in the work environment or more explicitly advocate the use of sports teams to generate social solidarity in the life of the commercial enterprise.

38 Allegiances to teams are both intense and persistent. A man in Colorado attempted suicide because *his* Denver Broncos fumbled the football too often. The *Broncos* were fumbling—and this man wanted to shoot *himself*. A man named Charlie Winkler follows the University of Nebraska football team all around the country. "Loudy" Loudensberger raises a Balti-

more Colt flag on his front lawn. Larry Hallenback, keeping up a family tradition, spends the night before every Kansas–Kansas State basketball game camped out in the cold outside Allen Fieldhouse so that he can be first inside. Roger Kahn lovingly describes his own involvement with the Brooklyn Dodgers from childhood to young adulthood, while diehard devotees still hold regular meetings of the St. Louis Browns Fan Club, a team that has been moribund for more than twenty-five years.

To understand the political importance of team symbolism, it is necessary to demonstrate how the team acts as a socializer of important values in American society while at the same time creating a dramatic, autonomous, and real "world" of its own. Failure to grasp the symbolic power of the team within the Sportsworld drama weakens any attempt to understand *how* values are internalized by masses of people. In turn, an analysis of sports as a symbolic world allows us to see how sports involvement can become a counterpoint to the decline of political allegiance and the widespread nostalgia for community in America.

The symbolic allure of the team rests on the aesthetic structure of the Sportsworld itself. Sports symbolism creates a "bracketed world" emotionally segregated from the everyday worlds that people inhabit; this is a powerful source of its appeal. The team plays a central role in this larger sports drama.

The Sportsworld, as a play-world, is an imaginary universe of living beings, but with a reality all its own. Lewis Cole captures the lively dramatic structure of the Sportsworld and the fan's central role, in his discussion of the drama of basketball:

39

Every contest is a drama of this conflict. Even before the play begins, while entering the arena, we know the basic plot. The players will try to fashion themselves into a flawless unit, and several stories will be enacted during the quest—a rookie's progress, a duel between two well-matched antagonists, one player's battle with age, another's combat with his own selfishness, a third's attempt to curb his frenzied enthusiasm. Sitting above the court, we are so intimate with the particulars of the story that we feel a strange identification with its protagonists, the players. We associate ourselves with their efforts, cheering and booing their performances, often even imagining ourselves part of the team; at the same time, we can't help them practically; they alone decide the story's end. Experiencing the acts of their performance is a double role, we talk about them using both "we" and "they" interchangeably.

Social order depends upon the creation of a symbolic canopy—or system of belief—that integrates everyday reality into a master plan. The strong normative structure of the Sportsworld is underscored in the struggle to make the team. This struggle is mediated by newspapers, magazines, and popular biographies and is integrated into everyday life through fan communication. The social emphasis that schools, communities, and media give to what Michael Novak calls the process of "election" dramatizes the prestige of the team and importance of adherence, like young monks, to the proven ways of devotion.

The young athlete learns the importance of self-discipline, the necessity of "guts" and mental toughness. He acquires a code that helps him form a strong personality to use in the competitive process. The code is strongly individualistic, emphasizes the control of emotions and the centrality of competition and winning. More important, this strongly individualistic code converges with the moral necessity of collective sacrifice. The slogan "There is no 'I' in *Team*" underscores this basic moral imperative. Children adopt these principles as they participate in the increasingly institutionalized junior leagues and as they feel the pressure to represent their communities in high school competition. As George

40

Kirk, assistant football coach at Baylor, remarks: "The Community *expects* a boy who's able to play to play. Football becomes important to him because it's important to the community."

The self-sacrifice to make the team and the collective sacrifice for the team's welfare accentuate the larger dramatic meanings. This is most clearly seen in sports fiction for children. In *The Kid from Tomkinsville,* young Roy Tucker worries about making the team:

He was not only unhappy, he was afraid, and his loneliness accentuated his fright. There was the fear of not making good, of having to return home without a job as everyone in Tomkinsville had predicted. Worst of all there was the worry as to whether he'd ever be able to return. Suppose he couldn't make the grade?

Once the struggles for election are resolved, the key question is whether the team will mesh as a unit. When cohesion is achieved, the powerful symbolism of collective struggle and the common good is dramatized. In John Tunis's *The Keystone Kids,* the point is clear:

A team is made up of equal parts of Bob's pep and fire and vinegar mixed with Roy's quiet determination when things went wrong. . . It was Karl Case's drive and push in the clutch when he forgot his batting average and was trying hard to win for the club. . . It was all these men and all these qualities that made a team.

The struggle to make the team and the effort to make the team mesh underscore the larger competitive drama between teams: the struggle to win. These struggles, the interweaving of plots, are brought to life by actors who give the plots human significance. It is crucial that the plots, characterizations, and beliefs take place within a clearly delineated hierarchy of authority. In keeping with the significantly human nature of the Sportsworld, authority is not heavily bureaucratic or impersonal. The commissioners who sit atop the structure are always personally involved in the doctrinal

41

disputes—settling "compensation" cases, overruling protests, and sometimes vetoing trades because they are not "in the best interests of the sport."

The owners of teams are not a faceless corporate elite but concerned leaders who anguish over defeat and visibly exult in victory. This comment on Chicago Bears' owner "Papa" George Halas is representative: "The old warrior fights his battles from a desk now but he is there all day every week day and half a day Saturday, the way everybody worked when the warrior was in his prime. And not puttering around you understand—working." Halas personally symbolizes the Bears' history, and his involvement with the team is dramatically portrayed during games. The eighty-two-year-old Papa Bear will not let anyone accompany him to a game, "lest he appear too coarse and obstreperous."

Sports ownership is also deeply immersed in the underlying plots of the sports drama. The newspapers and magazines focus on the decisions of concerned owners. The owner is portrayed as part businessman, part fan. In 1977, a protracted struggle between New York Met pitcher Tom Seaver and Met owner M. Donald Grant was played out in the newspapers with *Daily News* columnist Dick Young warring (on Grant's behalf) with New York *Post* columnist Maury Allen (fighting for Seaver). The part that Yankee owner George Steinbrenner played in the protracted battle between Reggie Jackson and Billy Martin is well known. As part of the drama the owner may be a person to identify with but he also receives abuse when the team consistently is disappointing. The Knickerbocker ownership has been frequently criticized for incompetence, while fan disgust and disillusionment led to nothing less than mutiny because of New York Giant owner Wellington Mara's handling of the team.

Further down the corporate hierarchy are the general managers and coaches whose day-to-day decisions decide the fate of the team. Scapegoating most often takes place on this

42

level. The coach especially becomes a ritual victim whose "sacking" strengthens the normative structure and social cohesiveness of the team. This is important because all order is based on a struggle between good and bad principles and people in which the guilty are purged and victimized through a dramatic ritual.

The entire social world of sports rests on a group infrastructure of professional, collegiate, scholastic, and junior league teams. The team acts as a symbolic community of sports. It is this feeling of community that connects people's everyday lives to belief systems and structures of authority. The group infrastructure gives the social bond its intensity and immediacy. The fans follow the team religiously throughout the season and read, hopefully, about its rebuilding efforts during the off season. This intensity of meaning is dramatized by Neal Offen:

I know of a doctor...who was told he was suffering from leukemia. He wasn't going to die immediately, but he was going to have to live with the knowledge of a disease that made death something more than abstract. The fear and the anxiety were so great that he was going to commit suicide. Then he became involved with the fortunes of a professional basketball team. The team started to have great success and the doctor decided against suicide. He decided—because of the way men unknown to him shoot and pass a round ball—that he was going to live.

The team is the backdrop for stories about the players themselves. We learn of their individual personalities and how they relate to their teammates and to authority. More important, their styles and personalities represent the team for the fan audience. Former Denver Bronco defensive end Lyle Alzado, with his frenzied enthusiasm, is an excellent example:

During a game Alzado emits waves of energy that radiate clear into the stands. On the field he never stops running...Off the field he

43

stalks the sidelines—talking, remonstrating, gesticulating...He pats heads with his huge bandaged forearms and roars with laughter when things are going well. When they are not, there is no one in the stadium more anguished.

This coincides with the fans' needs:

And Denver loves it. A young fan once wrote, "Dear Lyle, you are the meanest defensive end I have ever seen. The way you rip all those quarterbacks is terrific. I sure am glad you play for the Broncos."

This exemplifies the central importance of the game as the crucible of emotional identification. The symbolism of the team comes alive. The relationship between the fan and his or her team is solidified through dramatic confrontations. University of Kansas fans, for example, line up for tickets for the big game with Kansas State at 1:30 A.M.—in nine-degree weather! Kansas fans no longer may sit behind the opponent's bench because of their penchant for harassment.

The game generates intense emotions, and a common enemy creates community solidarity. John Tunis's fictional account of the game unifying players, teams, and fans is illustrative:

He could even distinguish voices in the roar.
"Go get 'em, Roy...!"
"You can do it, Tuck...!"
They knew him. And he knew them, through those terrible periods of July and August they had stayed behind the team; winning or losing, in rain or shine, wind, heat, they were always there. Here they were for the last game of all, his friends sticking with him to the end.

44

The identification with the team's struggle creates a euphoric togetherness, a merging of sensibilities. This euphoria makes the rational legal structure of the Sportsworld dramatic. The structure also is upheld by the arbiters of the sport. No matter how much fans complain about referees or umpires, their decisions are always accepted. Adhering to the rules makes victory sweet.

The team is the center of the Sportsworld's drama, but the language of sports is the symbolic glue that links people in taverns, offices, and car pools across the country. Sports talk is concrete, personal, and its cues are readily understood. Talking about the team becomes the core of everyday communication. There are traditional "watering holes" throughout the country where loyal fans gather before and after each game to discuss strategy, lay blame for defeat, and predict the future. One of the more notorious examples of this is the way the University of Kentucky basketball team dominates informal chatting throughout the entire state, "discussed avidly along with the price of tobacco and cattle." Talk about the team keeps the fire of solidarity burning long after the game ends and the fans must return to the more mundane tasks of everyday life.

Sports' dramatic symbols help create and maintain political cohesion, but only because the obstacles faced in sports closely reflect real-life problems. We must continually remember that important political and social values make an "end run" around conscious resistance through the sports drama. The Sportsworld caters to Americans' fantasies while simultaneously passing along the values of the political and social hierarchy. Through the glamour of sports, politically significant values are revered in an arena that is relatively free of political controversy. Because all political structures generate a good deal of tension when their sacred symbols and expectations become unrealistic, the sports drama, performing a ritual function, symbolically resolves such tension.

45

In attempting to bring to life the symbolism of the team, I have concentrated on team portrayals in various print media. I wanted to see if I could distill recurrent themes and images from this mass of documents. I used these media because I believe it is the reporter—in all his guises—who gives the game on the field human significance. Roger Kahn's confrontation with veteran sportswriter Dick Young emphasizes my point:

(Kahn): But most of the time you do write the games.
(Young): That's right, and when you do you forget the *Times*. They tell the score but the real fan knows the score already. When you do write the game, the way you do it is: "In yesterday's 3-2 Dodger victory the most interesting thing that happened was. . . Get that? Someone stole two bases. Someone made a horseshit pitch. Dressen made a mistake. Not just the score. Tell 'em fucking why or make them laugh. . ."

The sports reporter mediates the world; he assigns responsibilities, puts the game into dramatic form, and searches for the controversies and hidden meanings. The reporter makes the world of sports concrete and personal. He brings it to life in idyllic form because of his own involvement. Phil Berger's account of the idealization of the 1969–1970 New York Knicks clarifies what is operating here:

Writers felt an affection for the team [Sportswriter Augie Borgi named his son David William after Stallworth and Bradley] that limited barbed comments on players' ability. Sly [Berger's own persona] could understand it: after the close associations he'd had on road trips, he welcomed getting away from the players so that he could ponder them more objectively.

Berger describes how New York *Post* reporter Leonard Lewin would privately and sometimes publicly censor any copy he felt might damage the team. The excitement on the field and the demands of the fans for an engaged perspective push the reporter to become involved. The intense drama of the 1969–1970 Knick season, culminating in a series of inconceivably exciting play-offs, quickly stripped the veneer of objectivity from Berger himself. He tells of reading all the afternoon papers to psych *himself* up for an important game with the Bullets. He then describes what happened to him during the game: "And in the press box, Sly, who had sat objectively through a season's games, began to raise his fists at Knick baskets, and profane referees he had earlier interviewed."

The popular team sagas are even more intimate. George Plimpton's *Out of My League* and *Paper Lion* are models of these inside diaries. Plimpton wanted to provide his readers with a sense of what it was like to be *inside* a sports team. The books played out the fantasies and daydreams that so many people have about being a team member. This inside-dopester genre captures the human drama behind and within the game.

Many journalistic critics of sports decry the reporters' emotional involvement with the events they cover. This critical thrust is misplaced. The very structure of the Sportsworld and the nature of fan involvement create a demand for dramatic reporting. It is clear that any newspaper attempting to give fans "objective" reporting would rapidly lose its devoted sports section readers. It is for these reasons that controversial columnists like Dick Young, Larry Merchant, David Israel, and Jerry Izenberg and enthusiastically rabid announcers like Marv Albert and Johnny Most attract great followings. The dynamics at work here also explain Howard Cosell's huge popularity in the role of media villain. Villainy as well as heroism highlight the drama.

The media take us inside the intimate world of the team. It is helpful to think of the team as a model work community. The team symbolizes, on many levels, the hierarchy, specialization, and division of labor associated with the organized world of work. In the team imagery this is represented in the way certain people are praised as "unsung heroes." A player

47

like former Knick Mike Riordan is willing to come off the bench to "give a foul," to perform a menial task. For this he is lionized by his coach:

It is just as important for Mike Riordan to give a foul at the right time as it is for Willis Reed to score thirty-five points...I never had to explain to Riordan why he was being used mainly to give fouls. He did it because he felt it was important. It was his involvement with the team.

The symbolism of the division of labor can also be seen in the acclaim given the specialty teams in football, the praise heaped on those players who can substitute in key situations, and, as Jeff Greenfield illuminates in his paean to the Boston Celtics, how specialized tasks lead to winning play:

If there is one fundamental to be learned from the astonishing reign of the Boston Celtics, it is that a team wins when players are permitted to concentrate on their skills and forget about their weaknesses. Let the defensive specialists harass the opponent's best ballhandlers and shooters and reward them for what they do well...Tell your shooters to shoot. In other words look at the game of basketball as a series of necessary skills that can be scattered among your team—as long as one player possesses an essential skill of extremely high quality.

Another essential characteristic of organization is skilled leadership—an ability to be an expert strategist as well as an efficient handler of people. In almost every article on a team in *Sports Illustrated* over a two-year period (1975-1977), the expertise and leadership qualities of owners, general managers, and coaches are prominently mentioned as essential to team success. All these articles, and the books that focus specifically on coaches, emphasize the psychological skills of emotional management as a prerequisite for success.

The coach must have the ability to personally mold the team in his image and forge the social skills necessary for success; owners are praised for their visibility and personal concern. The personal and communal are grafted onto the functional and organizational. This parallels the shift in organizational ideology in this century from an emphasis on impersonal, autocratic control to the stressing of humane, personal, and social-psychological leadership skills.

The concern is with *morale* and the fear is of disorganization. Even when sports authority remains autocratic, as it does in some areas of football, it is softened by a personal warmth and concern. The two primary models of this are Woody Hayes and the late Vince Lombardi. One of Lombardi's former players illustrates the way he used to get the team "up" through the force of his personality:

Lombardi turned and faced us. "OK, boys," he began, then stopped and rubbed his hands together for several seconds . . . "This may be the last time we'll be together so, uh . . . " His lips actually began to tremble, his whole body quivered. He looked like he was about to start bawling. He never finished the sentence . . . I don't think any of us concentrated on the film; we were all wondering what playing for Green Bay would be like without Lombardi. *It's been hell to play while he's been here, but I don't want to play if he's not around.*

Authority in sports is concrete and personal. The humaneness through the poignant tears of a street-tough Al McGuire when he wins a college basketball championship shows just prior to his retirement. It likewise flows from such hardboiled coaches as George Allen (in a tearful press conference), Red Auerbach (emotionally embracing a tear-streaked Bob Cousy), and John Wooden (his reserve discarded in an embrace with star UCLA player Sidney Wicks).

Personal authority and intimacy, when successfully combined, lead to the creation of a cohesive team order. Team morale is aided by effective leadership but is expressed in the close working relations of the players. The potentially divisive effects of the division of labor are overcome by the intimacy of the locker room and the collective pursuit of common objectives. Also, added solidarity is created because

49

the players need to put up a united front in order to enhance the effectiveness of the team. This leads players to regard each other as co-conspirators and to protect their own individual and collective image vis-à-vis the press and the public. Phil Berger catches this in an anecdote about the Knicks:

The stories that Barnett recounted were not to his thinking society's possessions. "I call what I got inside humour!" He said, "Some of it is for the ballplayers and nobody else to hear" . . . He maintained in locker-rooms the inscrutable front of a sphinx save for those moments when the doors were barred to outsiders.

This solidarity is by no means entirely contrived. The team does spontaneously enact a certain kind of warmth and intimacy that is palpable to players and fans alike. Bill Bradley eloquently captures this:

The lockerroom had become a kind of home to me. . . I often enter tense and uneasy, disturbed by some event of the day. Slowly my worries fade as I see their unimportance to my male peers. I relax, my concerns lost *among relationships that are warm and real but never intimate,* lost among the constants of an athlete's life. Athletes may be crude and immature but they are genuine when it comes to loyalty. The lines of communication are clear and simple. . . we are at ease in the setting of satin uniforms and shower nozzles.

George Plimpton and Jim Bouton in *Ball Four* also talk about this special form of male intimacy that is "warm and real but never intimate." The life in such a work community is never totally stable—players are "cut" and traded. While they remain together, however, they reach a level of fellowship that is perhaps only approached during civil disasters and wartime. It is not the anonymous closeness of the crowd. In *Paper Lion,* Plimpton describes the storytelling and pranks of training camp in a tone that brings to mind the vivid camaraderie of male urban street life—the playing of dominoes or poker out in the streets of working-class neighborhoods.

50

In reading the literature on teams I began to see some important parallels between the players' sense of togetherness and the models of fraternity developed by Carey McWilliams. McWilliams emphasizes the importance of male bonds and indicates their democratizing power. No discussion of the sports team or American sports symbolism in general can fail to come to grips with sports' historic role as a refuge for male warmth and meaning. Teams often are closeted in ascetic school dormitories away from their families during training camp, and during the season take long road trips. The anonymity of the road often thrusts players into the warmth of male friendship. Bradley illustrates this in his description of his relationship with Dave DeBusschere:

There is much in our relationship that is left unspoken, but it is hard to imagine it ending. Living together makes for a strong bond...shared toiletries, mutual kidding...Sometimes we keep our luggage in the same room in a town and never see each other. But this is precisely what is good about our friendship. There is no need to feel guilty for not socializing together every night on the road...Within the boundaries of that friendship there is much room for good times, affection and deep respect.

The male intimacy of the team, in contrast with all male socialization patterns outside sports, also is warmly physical. The team—as a symbol of masculine cooperation—is far enough beyond suspicion to allow "unmasculine" emotions to be cultivated. The warmly physical intimacy also transcends racial barriers. Rugged (and white) Dave DeBusschere runs into the Knickerbocker locker room after their 1970 championship victory, embraces the 6'10", 260-pound Willis Reed, and plants a kiss on his cheek. This interracial male intimacy is vividly symbolized during the games. Players hug each other after home runs or touchdowns, pat each other on the behind, and affectionately slap palms after key baskets or goals.

The team synthesizes powerful egos into an organized whole. In many ways it captures the spirit of the ancient community but in the context of the modern reality of individual personality. It symbolically integrates individual personality and collective ideals. There is the warmth of intimate cooperation *and* the structure of statuses and authority. There is joy *and* work. These elements are combined successfully because the team has a sense of purpose, which culminates for players and fans alike in the euphoria of the victorious locker room. This ecstasy in victory gives all the prior painful self-discipline and momentary setbacks meaning. The team effort captures and portrays the aesthetic ideals of craftsmanship and communion and infuses the division of labor in a "festival of common delight."

The athlete receives immense ego gratification for his performance. This participation in a shared celebration intensifies the social bond between teammates and coaches. Jerry Kramer gives insight into this moment:

Greg and I, the two men closest to the coach, just lifted him up and started running out on the field. He was grinning at us and slapping us and he hollered. "Head for the dressing room, boys..." We finished the Lord's Prayer and we all began slapping each other on the back and hugging each other once again...I wanted to keep my uniform on as long as I possibly could.

In this sense, teams like the Green Bay Packers, the Boston Celtics, and the old New York Yankees are the Sportsworld's models that establish the values and goals of the arena. Their appeal extends beyond the Sportsworld itself. The team becomes a "metaphor for ultimate cooperation."

52   In the sense that order rests on disorder, these model teams stand in contrast to the strife-torn negative team models. To know the joys of cooperation we must learn the evils of dissension and discord. The appeal of the hero is dramatized through the villainy of his opponent. During the Knicker-

bocker championship year, the New York *Post* frequently focused on the problems of the visiting teams in articles such as "Are the Rockets Ready to Fire Their Coach?" and "The Glory That Was Boston." These stories highlighted the fragility of team morale, its dependence on effective leadership, and the necessity for ample amounts of self-sacrifice.

The models of failure are highlighted by the grousing of malcontented players, the inefficiency of too weak or too harsh and remote coaches, and the jarring interventions of irascible team owners. In focusing on a successful team, *Sports Illustrated* habitually underscores how the new team leadership is effectively overcoming the patterns of past failure. All of the sagas written on the Knick championship pay much attention to the failure of the previous coach to maintain a purposeful discipline and how Coach Red Holzman turned that around. These chronicles also relate how former players Walt Bellamy and "Butch" Komives, through their inability to sacrifice themselves for the team, disrupted it. Their departure is seen as the first step—a necessary ritual victimage—toward the creation of team solidarity.

Aside from the central importance of the coach, the two most important factors contributing to dissension are "enlarged egos" and "high-priced superstars." The rise of Big Money is a definite threat to the structure of sports. Reporters, acting as gatekeepers of sports' value system, look for and often find discord on teams whose successes were engineered through crass cash purchases. The past controversies surrounding the Philadelphia 76ers in basketball and the New York Yankees in baseball dramatize the media's function as watchdog. The press's role is to maintain vigilance by highlighting the forces of disharmony.

53

Team harmony, like order in the Sportsworld in general, is created through drama. The drama is both internal and external as if focusing on the dynamics of the team and the competition between teams. For each team the season is a lifetime, replete with successes, defeats, joys, humiliations, and symbolic rebirths. The beginning of the new season is marked by sacrifice symbolizing the change from off-season sloth to in-season dedication. The fan is drawn into the seasonal rebirth—the charley horses, sore arms, bruised heels, and separated shoulders.

The drama is made poignant by the publicized struggle to make the team. Invariably we read of some rookie who has sacrificed a good job possibility merely for the chance to make the team. The desire to gain election leads to intense mortification, as in the case of the New York Jets' Greg Murphy, a free agent making a third try to escape the pathos of East New York who collapsed from heat exhaustion during training camp. We appreciate the honor of being *chosen* and the self-abnegation of those who seek glory. As fans, we are also imbued with the team's purpose, symbolically transformed into a life or death struggle. As Jim Bouton and others have pointed out, when a player is cut it is said, "He died."

Preseason is a time of sacrifice that perhaps will lead to the eventual redemption of a World Series or a Super Bowl. The season itself takes on a dramatic quality of its own. It may be characterized by the bickering failings of a loser or the festive communion of a winner—or both. Each game contains parallel dramas. Defeat or a losing season may be imminent, yet "it's never over till the last out."

George Allen says defeat is worse than death because you have to live with defeat. In a sense this is true. If winning is a life tonic, then losing is surely a deathlike witch's brew. When losing becomes endemic for a franchise, the pain the fans feel can eventually resemble a tyrannical oppression. If the humiliation extends over years, the hope of redemption becomes as elusive as the revivalist's promise of "milk and

54

honey on the other side." In this context the diehard fan will often, like the downtrodden slave, think negatively of himself because of his team's defeats.

This is why each game is presented in military terms and why the local papers are full of agitation about the opposition's mean or awesome characteristics. The game is the crucible that determines how well the team has followed the Sportsworld's imperatives.

Defeat leads to doubt and the search for an explanation. Media scrutiny magnifies the first rumblings of discontent, which then takes on a life of its own. The players usually are criticized, but the coach is held responsible. The coach serves as an exquisite ritual victim for the team's frustrated fans. Through the building drama of outrage—"Martin Teeters on the Brink"—the "causes" of disorder are rooted out. The media's crucial role is underscored by the calm exhibited by the normally tumultuous New York Yankees during the newspaper strike in the summer of 1978.

Ritual victims rarely are actually at fault. Player selfishness, mismanagement by the ownership, "bad breaks" are all part of the make-up of defeat. The "canning" of the coach appeases the fans and expiates the players' guilt. The team is both let off the hook and shamed for its part in the ritual slaughter. The players bind together and vow to uphold the authority of the new coach. The fans also realize, post hoc, that the coach couldn't have been the only one to blame, but with their anguish expunged, their hope is renewed.

The dramatic nature of fan-team involvement is epitomized by the saga of the 1969–1970 New York Knickerbockers. Knick fans, as my introduction attests, suffered through over two decades of humiliation. As that championship season approached, the fans wondered if their suffering would finally end. The anticipation of redemption built over a magnificent eighteen-game winning streak. After the old hated rivals, the Boston Celtics, were soundly trounced,

55

Celtic Coach Tom Heinsohn accurately observed, "It must be sweet for the Knicks, after we sat on their fannies for so many years. . ." It wasn't, however, the current players who had suffered. It was the fans. The players participate in an ongoing drama that is defined for them before they join the team. They learn about the team's history and become its representatives. The fans' own involvement can easily span an entire lifetime. Childhood identifications extend into adulthood and old age—an impressive example of continuity in an age of dislocation.

An adequate political theory of American sports must grasp the interaction between sports as a socializer and sports as a symbolic refuge. Team symbolism underscores this subtle interaction quite clearly. Initially, America's dominant team sport was baseball. The rise of baseball coincides with the post–Civil War period of modernization that was characterized by rapid industrialization, urbanization, and democratization. The potential for widespread social upheaval was furthered by an influx of the foreign-born, uprooted from alien cultures and traditional social orders. Participation in sports was encouraged by concerned elites as part of the overall process of "Americanization."

The immigrants were crowded into urban ghettos where "pathology" of all kinds flourished. The immigrants were linked in the native American mind with crime, perversion, and radicalism. Baseball became an excellent way for the newcomer to escape moral censure. The folk understanding saw the game as a "builder of character." It was felt sports developed the desirable social character traits that would benefit American society. Sports was seen as American and moral: "Sports have supplied a new and effective motive for resisting all sins which can corrupt the body and the nation."

The team was seen to foster the ideals of honorable struggle and fair play, which, it was felt, translated into the

56

language of self-government and good citizenship. This theory was most vividly formulated by George Herbert Mead, who saw the team as a particularly effective vehicle of initial socialization in a democracy. He also saw it as a model for the secondary socialization of adults into a community of equals because of its emphasis on equality. We can see this clearly in Hugh Duncan's discussion of Mead's analysis of games:

As he plays his own position, the player guides himself by his ability to arouse within himself responses and attitudes that arise in those who play other positions. Players on a team are related in an organized and unitary fashion. The responses of the players are predictable in terms of rules which all know and agree to. When conflict arises, the umpire is given power to make decisions. He is the actor whose role personifies the "generalized other." In him, universal and highly abstract rules come to life in action.

This one ritual drama contains a community of equals, the division of labor, the idea of cooperative work, an emphasis on competition, and the legal-rational structure of authority. As Reuel Denney observes, "The artificial time and space limits of the game permit fluid interpersonal experience that would never occur so rapidly or with such permutations in real life." So while real-life competition is enervating and the rules often are quite rigid, the game allows a genuine sense of fairness to flourish. The harshness of the attack on the critical tendency of political elites to rhetorically transpose norms of "sportsmanship," "rules of the game," and "fair play" to real-life situations merely underscores the political and social impact of the game.

Two factors enhance the force of these socialization patterns. In the first place, the process takes place at an early age and occurs in the atmosphere of happy playing. Secondly, sports' appeal rests on the sense that it is "above politics." The larger society uses this apolitical "mystery" of sports to decorate its own hierarchical structure. This process of transposing values from one realm to another can be glimpsed in this way: "Baseball is a Lockean game, a kind of contract theory in ritual form, a set of atomic individuals who assent to patterns of limited cooperation in their mutual interest."

This socialization drama is not static but follows historical patterns. The "Lockean game" dominated the early era of American capitalism—a period of hard work, competition, and individualism. The development of American capitalism confronted the myth of Horatio Alger with new institutional realities. Large-scale political, social, and economic bureaucracies began to challenge the credibility of individualism and the cohesion of small-town life.

With the rise of factory and city, with the specialization and rationalization of work and society, widespread concern arose over the threat of disorganization and political disruption. A whole range of social scientists began to worry over the growing specter of anomie caused by capitalist development. Mead and others vividly saw the need to infuse capitalist society with an aesthetic sense of purpose that would provide the "shared experiences" necessary to overcome the isolating currents of the division of labor. Mead's choice of team-game symbolism for his communal model is illuminating. The team and its purposes shine with a clarity the rest of society lacks, enabling the values of social cooperation to be extended to the society at large.

The emerging bureaucratic reality led to the evolution of a new "social ethic." The decline of rugged individualism and the rise of a "new mythology" of group predominance, "togetherness," and "belongingness" was a major shift in American ideology. The new emphasis gave rise to industrial psychology and human relations experts. This movement, led by Elton Mayo and his colleagues at the Harvard Business School, attacked the disciples of Frederick Taylor, who had emphasized the technical rationalization of the firm. They

58

pointed out that this form of rationalization failed to under-stand the worker as a person enmeshed in a web of social relations. The new approach emphasized the factory as a social system. Mayo and his colleagues saw the need to create a sense of morale through a more effective integration of the individual into the social processes of the factory.

The human relations approach centered around the idea of teamwork. The dual emphasis was on creating a *sense* of teamwork in the process of work itself and on the creation of sports *teams*. The purpose was to break down potential class conflict and imbue workers with a sense of belonging to the entire "community." The key to this approach's success was the training of administrators with "social skills" who created more effective "communication" and "cooperation."

The creation of an administrative elite to facilitate political and social integration completely (and often deliberately) by-passes the political process. A democratic society wrangles about the aims of integration and cooperation. The ideology of administrative integration, however, operates differently. The group theories of human relations ignore the need for debate and political conflict. For them, group cohesion is to be achieved through the techniques of integration.

The entire thrust of industrial psychology dramatizes a popular form of apolitical politics. If the organization is a social system, there is no reason for the absence of democratic debate and political struggle. The image of "social system," however, implies a stable structure of statutes similar to the hierarchy that existed in the middle ages, a time when individuals were *rooted* in a stable social order. In fact, this is Mayo's ideal imagery. It is the marriage of an old dowager to a young stud. The hierarchical roles of Plato's *Republic* are bolstered by the techniques of scientific human management.

This aversion to politics as too remote, uncertain, and divisive became quite prevalent. The twentieth-century mani-festation of this "sublimation of politics" emphasizes the need

59

to induce a sense of community within the very bowels of the organization. "Society" (the factory) must fulfill the person's emotional needs through the provision of a cohesive moral order. If "society" fails to do this, disorder and chaos will result.

The apolitical politics of integration amounts to an arbitrary redefinition of democracy. If left to themselves, the mass of people will allow their "antisocial" or "neurotic" natures to explode into "morbid" forms of radical politics. The people are desperately in need of guidance. This idea is vividly formulated in Mayo's discussion of radicalism. Mayo tells the story of a radical student leader who was persuaded to go to a psychiatrist, and who soon afterward discarded his "neurosis-induced" political activity. Writers in this tradition are quick to associate radicalism with psychopathology.

Mayo also felt that absenteeism, strikes, and sabotage were caused by the failure of administrators to instill the ideal of teamwork. The point must be emphasized again that the ideology of teamwork and cooperation ("getting along"), rising to the level of a moral imperative, is a form of mysticism that obscures the vital question of what the *goals* of teamwork should be.

It is quite clear that the sports team meshes with the goals of administrative capitalism. It is no accident that as American society became more complex and bureaucratic, the more corporate games of football and basketball rose to popularity. It is a mistake, however, made by Jeff Greenfield and Michael Novak, to view this development as a form of socialism. The goals of social cooperation, integration, and collective purpose, far from being necessarily socialistic, were precisely those goals articulated by Emile Durkheim, a man who spent his entire career devising moral alternatives to socialism and social conflict. The team and its coach symbolize these conflict-free features.

The team, besides acting as an agent of socialization, can also be seen as a symbolic refuge from many ills that are endemic to capitalist society. Foster Rhea Dulles observed this in the rise of baseball. He saw the appeal of baseball linked to the closing of the frontier and the process of urbanization. "America had discovered a new world," Dulles wrote, and that world existed as a pastoral retreat from the crowding and evils of city life. The world of baseball began to be seen as a moral world above the corruption of the urban political landscape. This *moral* sports/*immoral* politics dichotomy was dramatized in the 1919 Black Sox scandal, where the tampering with the World Series produced a sense of moral outrage that far transcended the tempest over the Teapot Dome.

The use of the sports team as a symbolic refuge became more important with the entrenchment of the industrialization-bureaucratization process. There is a tendency for political, economic, and social processes to become "reified," seemingly fixed and frozen beyond human control. The world of capitalism becomes a "natural world" that people feel helpless in confronting.

In this context authority becomes remote, abstract, and formal. The individual finds it difficult to relate positively to the state. Organizations are equally ill equipped to provide emotional nurturance because they are too instrumental and bureaucratic. It is within this climate that the "quest for community" becomes a political issue. The institutional structure no longer seems to possess a human content and people begin to search for human significance in the private order.

Individuals are forced to seek sustenance on their own when institutions offer little emotional support. Warmth and communal meaning are an important aspect of this search for identity. Much of this searching, though, features an un-

61

avoidable instability. The proliferation of avenues open to individuals makes the identity process purely subjective. Freedom coexists with uncertainty, and "homelessness" is a permanent feature of this society.

The Sportsworld as a social life-world and the team symbolism of community, fraternity, and intimacy stand in vivid counterpoint to developments in the "real" world. The symbolic-aesthetic appeals of sports are warmly personal and concrete. The Sportsworld contains what the real world lacks: charisma, magical performances, gifted leaders, and intense rituals.

Involvement in the Sportsworld contrasts sharply with the withdrawal and wary cynicism characteristic of the American citizen. This dichotomy is drawn effectively in the sagas of J. Henry Waugh and Frederick Exley. Waugh, the protagonist of Robert Coover's *The Universal Baseball Association, Inc.,* is a browbeaten accountant, uninvolved in either his work or meaningful social relations. He creates a fictional baseball world by rolling dice and compiling statistical ledgers. He lives out the games and the personal lives of the players. As his involvement with his fabricated world increases, his attachment to his "real" world lessens. Eventually, Waugh appears to have a "psychotic break" and permanently takes up residence in his "Universal Baseball Association."

In *A Fan's Notes,* Frederick Exley can't seem to function normally and is slowly losing his grip on "reality." He sees little sense in any of the traditional institutions (his marriage ends, for example) and even less in the various asylums he spends time in. The only thing that allows him to keep a grasp on "reality" is his attachment to the football Giants and Frank Gifford. They give him a "feeling of being alive." Frank Gifford becomes his "life raft." Toward the end of the book, Exley quits fighting his fate, abandons his dreams of personal fame, and accepts his destiny as a *fan*. The distance from J. Henry Waugh and Frederick Exley to the rest of us is a matter

62

of degree. Madness here provides evidence of normal involvement.

Intense involvement with the Sportsworld leads to yet another political ramification. Jürgen Habermas's investigation into legitimation in advanced capitalist society is important here. He sees the growing power of the "technical life-world" penetrating the social life-world of human meaning. With this technical penetration, it becomes increasingly difficult for people to actively control the directions of technological "progress."

The direction of technology remains in the hands of certain dominant interests. Democratic control can only occur if a democratic public is able to discuss issues knowledgeably and articulate a vision of the future. This possibility is frustrated by a process of depoliticization that rests on the seemingly autonomous nature of science and technology and the delivery of consumer goods. Substantive political questions are eliminated through the process of depoliticization: "the public realm loses its political function."

America's political legitimacy rests on a foundation of technological dominance and private consumption. While sports involvement reflects the rise of consumption, it has a life force and autonomy all its own. It feeds depoliticization by creating a world of meaning, a utopian refuge, within the larger technical life-world. The possibilities of political change are silenced by the din of the sports fans' time-honored cry of hope: "Wait till next year!"

4. "It's Only a Game": The Importance of Sports in Political Socialization

"The Yankee resurrection is as much a celebration of the past as the present. It has given the fans the purest of opportunities: the opportunity to turn back the clock and relive their childhoods. Or at least to feel they are reliving them."

Larry Schwartz

MY CHILDHOOD memories of sports are vivid, often blocking out entirely the events and characters of the real world. As I watch my favorite teams or as I continue to try to perfect my left-handed drive to the basket against children who have grown old, I am continually pulled back into an earlier, less problematic time. When Reggie Jackson hits that timely blast into the right-field bleachers and struts around the bases, memories return of punchball in the street, where hitting the "no parking" sign meant an automatic home run. When Earl Monroe "double-pumps" in a crowd, I am drawn back into the dingy gyms of childhood and adolescence where my life took shape and my identity was formed.

Clearly seeing the subtle connections between the world of children's play and games and the involvement of adults in the Sportsworld drama is the key toward understanding the deep-seated personal and political implications of sports in America. John Mosedale citing Wilfred Sheed gives us a worthy pregame analysis:

"If you had to limit yourself to one aspect of American life, the showdown between the pitcher and the hitter, quarterback and defense would tell you more about politics, manners, and style in this country than any one thing. . ." Sheed also warns that playing games can be "incurably childish." *Well, inside of every adult male is a little boy struggling to stay there.*

In many ways my father underscored the importance of the Sportsworld for me. This is where I got a glimpse of his real

65

strength—apart from the badgering of a domesticity he needed but was unable to cope with calmly. The sagas of his own athletic past spurred my search for a solid male identity. In talking about his quarter-mile triumphs his whole being would come alive. This was a place where men could triumph and escape the restrictive world of work and home. I caught the intense feeling of "all this was very important to me," even in the stories of his run-ins with insensitive coaches. I was transported back with him in the spirit of camaraderie. To this day he continues to retell these tales; they are the sacred myths of his life. As I listened to him, searching for maleness and a greater closeness to him, I began the voyage whose myths I am now recounting.

My father's stories were just a part of his influence. We watched the Knicks, the Yankees, and the football Giants together. Although he was never a great fan, his concern with taking *me* (my sister was excluded most of the time) overcame his emotional distance from the event. Track meets, however, were different. Here he was involved; his whole world of meaning and triumph was re-created before his eyes, as well as mine. He would point out the different strides of the runners, talk excitedly about finishing kicks, and come alive—be happy—in ways I never otherwise saw. I could not have received a more vivid lesson about what was important in life.

I never did develop my father's love of running. I needed a distinct identity. Basketball became the focus of my life. Every evening of my adolescence my devotion was rededicated in the gyms and community centers around Manhattan. Despite my short size at the time—5'1" in junior high—I persevered in developing a jump shot that could be released quickly, perfecting my moves and learning to drive to the basket without being served up a "Spalding breakfast."

My Sportsworld refuge was not filled with unrestricted joy. If things hadn't gone well at home or at school and if feelings began to overflow and affect my real world activities, the gym or court became a safe place to work those feelings out. This need to escape placed a heavy burden on my refuge, because the playground was a struggle, a conflict where the stakes were pride, self-esteem, and personal identity. A "bad" series of games (my own critique was often much harsher than anyone else's) would often send me home in a state of gloom, agonizing over shots that were blocked or passes that were stolen and analyzing my weaknesses. Often, however, I would slump dejectedly into the sideline warmth of the lively discussions of games present, past, and future, and my gloom would be transformed in the acceptance of my status as a *player*.

My religious devotion, my mortification, sacrifice, and the sense of redemption I felt as my ability increased was crucial in this period. Adolescence often is a time when young people are willing to undertake all sorts of idealistic commitments. It is a time of painful awkwardness and uncertainty when youngsters sacrifice so much in order to build identity and find purpose in life. My own adolescence was typical in this respect. My adult future was dimly perceived and my adolescent present was painful. I feared sex and dating. I began to doubt the very masculinity I was seeking in the Sportsworld. The doubts and fears were compounded by a delayed puberty. It was a vicious cycle that threatened to sink my timorous sense of self-esteem. As adolescent navigation grew tougher, sports became my life raft.

Self-sacrifice and the goal of making my high school team consumed my life. As things grew tougher in everyday life, sports' mythological portrayal of the eventual reward for painful effort and perseverance gave me hope. I internalized the values in pursuit of my personal Holy Grail. When friends ridiculed my quest to make the team—I was a 5'4" sophomore in high school—my determination just became stronger. I wore weights on my ankles to improve my jumping. I played every day of the week. I was a zealot. In my senior year—I had zoomed up to 5'7"—I felt I was ready. I tried out for the team. After the second week of tryouts the team roster was posted on the bulletin board. My name seemed to jump off the wall in large neon letters. The larger possibility of achievement and success was personally confirmed in my own sports microsphere.

My personal struggles during adolescence took place within the warm confines of fellowship. This warmth was dramatized for me by the interracial character of my basketball community. Basketball in the early sixties was a city game that was rapidly becoming all black. It was a time before the bitter anger of the urban riots had exploded and my participation in a game that is a way of life in the black community pushed aside my outward suspicion or hostility. I would walk into gyms and be greeted by a sea of black faces. A moment's curiosity would fade, the game would continue, and performance became one's true measure.

Playing on a "Y" team accentuated this interracial acceptance. Joking and laughing with Perry Elliot, Rodney Butler, and Earl Manigault provided a warm scenic backdrop to my trials. As an adolescent I felt somewhat like an outcast and in the world of basketball I found acceptance with America's own outcasts and perhaps envisioned a different kind of world beyond the reality of racism outside. I will never forget crossing the street at night with Perry, Rodney, Duke, and a white Phil Stutz. All of a sudden Phil waded into traffic waving his arms and yelled, "Stop! Stop! 'Negro' crossing." The playful head-slapping and verbal abuse that followed confirmed and reinforced the special community we had created.

68

The interracial world of our own playing was intertwined with the larger integrated world of basketball in the city and throughout the country. We traveled to official and unofficial games to watch the best players and discuss their relative merits. If we did get polarized along racial lines (NYU's Jewish Barry Kramer versus NYU's black "Happy" Hairston), some cult figure like Connie Hawkins would solidify our New York chauvinism and common love for the game. In the process, our own playing, watching, talking, and fantasizing began to link us to a larger universe even as it cemented our own smaller personal world together.

As I grew up, the plots, scenes, heroes, and rituals of the Sportsworld became an integral part of my life. They gave me a distinct identity and a larger purpose that took me outside my own narrow universe. And as I began to ponder my own involvement and the involvement of so many others, it became clear that devotion to sports is probably the single most passionate attachment in America. My focus on childhood deepened my appreciation of this passion and clarified the political importance of the Sportsworld.

Political stability does not have to rest on the inculcation of a specific political ideology. It can have an even stronger foundation in the diffuse attachments that are generated in the activities of everyday life. We can appreciate this idea from the following illustration:

Dear Abby: About Amy who is going to marry a sports nut: I hope she reconsiders. I am married to such a man and it is awful! He lives for sports. The minute he opens his eyes in the morning he runs out to get the paper so he can look at the sports page. At breakfast there's no conversation since he is carefully reading the sports section. During our lovemaking he's listening to some game on the radio.

A seemingly apolitical symbol system that creates a diffuse "rain or shine" attachment to American culture can have an even more profound stabilizing effect than a concerted program of political propaganda. After all, a sense of national identity legitimizes the activities of political elites.

Throughout our lives, we tend to generalize from our

69

concrete and familiar surroundings to the more abstract notion of the political community. This "halo effect" insures political stability and prevents small flare-ups from becoming crises of legitimacy. During the Vietnam war, when I was threatened with military service in what I considered an irrational adventure, I thought about expatriation. I hesitated when I began to wonder how I would ever be able to follow the rising fortunes of my beloved New York Knickerbockers. Getting the New York *Post* delivered was not the ideal way to hide out from the authorities, and the irony of listening to the exploits of Willis Reed and Walt Frazier on Armed Forces Radio eluded me completely. America's hold on me was tighter than I had realized.

As the Sportsworld slowly seeps into our pores creating a personal love, it constructs a network for national and social communication. This "we-ness" begins at an early age and is nonrational and nonpolitical. Ghetto star and street philosopher Willie Hall makes this point: "There's a love of the game in this city that is very difficult to put into words. You start off when you're very young and you never quite get it out of your system. You might get married to a woman, but basketball is your first love."

This love and network of communication becomes the basis for a national identity and forms the foundation for political integration. Baseball historian Robert Smith captures this interweaving of personal, historical, and political themes:

Thus our love for the game grew deep, even when we were no more than mediocre performers. And we stumbled along from worse to better, learning the game *as the nation itself learned it,* first as an individual contest with each man playing the part awarded to him . . . then as a coordinated team contest with every member trying to work in unison with all the rest.

As my own story illustrates, I slowly emerged from my

70

personal world of home, street, and school into the larger universe of the Sportsworld. The values of this world became the foundation for my own identity. And as I have pointed out in the introduction, the values of the Sportsworld exist within the larger "shared vision" of American society. The Sportsworld functions like the world of the fairy tale: "Because it promises that the Kingdom will be his, the child is willing to believe the rest of what the fairy tale teaches."

The Sportsworld also allows for the discharge of painful emotions, which is an important facet of political stability. The ritual release of tension allows individuals space for individual growth, while at the same time it gives structure, form, and meaning to social life.

The worlds of play, games, and then sports cleanse the emotions precisely because as we enter them we feel we are leaving the real world behind. This seeming departure allows for the suspension of disbelief that enables political and social learning to take place.

As I witnessed the miracles and heroics of my Yankees, read analogous exploits in the Chip Hilton sports stories, and struggled to develop my own athletic skills, I easily internalized the myths of the larger society and struggled to hone those character traits that would insure my successful enactment of those myths.

My political education proceeded "latently" and "analogously." In the *Republic,* Plato hypothesized a plan for political education that would begin in childhood and utilize myths, fables, stories, and songs. It was important, he felt, to nurture the soil in which the sapling grows in order to avoid redirecting the tree later on.

Political and social institutions can only operate efficiently if personality traits of individuals mesh with the roles and structures of the society's institutions. This crucial development of a common social character has been especially important in the American context of immigration and rapid

71

economic expansion. The Sportsworld, as we shall see throughout this chapter, has been a conservative bulwark against the destructive force of political, social, and economic upheaval.

The cultivation of a common character was accomplished in part by the process of ethnic identification. Through this process, immigrants and their offspring could momentarily escape the rigors of the factories and the righteousness of the pulpits and share their sense of cultural dislocation with one another. At the same time, Sportsworld identifications were gradually and unwittingly inculcating the American ethos. Martin Ralbovsky's depiction of Schenectady's Italians illustrates the process at work:

Baseball, too, was making inroads with the old immigrants' sons; the reason was a centerfielder who played for the New York Yankees, Joe DiMaggio. Men whose grandfathers had toiled in the fields of Naples would sit next to radios, listening to an Alabamian named Melvin Israel (it was Mel Allen by then) describe the play-by-play of Yankee games in that honeysweet drawl of his. Whenever Joe DiMaggio came up to bat, life would come to a grinding halt on Flockie Boulevard and on Goose Hill; Italian men would yell out to their noisy families, "Hey a Joe Dee Maj ees up, now—a shed-op, or I whip-a you esses."

When I began to probe the centrality of childhood in the growth of the Sportsworld and, likewise, the growth of my own devotion, the year 1955 became pivotal. Whitey Ford pitched the season opener against the old Washington Senators that year, and the Yankees won 19-1 in an exciting display of power that fed my growing enchantment. I remember my family's first TV arrived a few weeks before the 1955 World Series. Before 1955: nothing; I drew a blank. I couldn't get past that year. Just when it appeared that my sports passion arose spontaneously, I found a clue in the biographies of the athletes themselves. All those stories were grounded in the imagery of play. I studied the extensive

72

literature on play and games and began searching for the theoretical connections all the popular accounts took for granted.

The theoretical accounts demonstrated that both play and games rest on the same foundations. Both have a symbolic form that separates them from the activities of everyday life. This symbolic separateness facilitates the feeling—the player is "possessed"—of escape from reality. This separateness, however, exists in an often unseen tension with the conflicts of the real world. Play and games emerge from and affect that larger reality.

Like the Sportsworld, the worlds of play and games represent the real world in a more manageable way. The child's play and games are *re-creations*, precisely because they re-create symbolically the society of which they are an integral part. The play activity of my daughter, Katie, age four, is illustrative. Katie went to the store on Fire Island with her seven-year-old brother, Jonathan, and his friend Seth. Following her own inclinations she smartly lifted a water-melon stick from the candy counter. By the time she arrived home Seth and Jonathan had made her feel as morally suspect as Jack the Ripper. Unable to take any more preaching she angrily screamed: "Stop splaining it to me, you splained it five times already and that's enough." Later on that week I overheard Katie in her room lecturing her "Dressie Bessie" with great glee about the evils of larceny.

It is precisely the dramatic nature of communication in play and games that helps internalize the larger issues. The drama of these symbolic worlds permits the discharge of painful emotions (Dressie Bessie takes over for Katie's own guilt) while allowing the smooth acceptance of the shared visions of the larger society ("Thou Shalt Not Steal"). Katie's ability to fantasize and navigate her ego between the micro-spheres and the larger reality is a key part of the process. The guilt, fears, and frustrations are externalized and she gains

73

a sense of mastery over her inner universe. She can then proceed to create order in her own life. Katie emerged from her room, smiling a "Hi Daddy" at me, refreshed as a sleeper from a dream that "worked."

The Sportsworld, as my own testimony underscores, lies at the end of a developmental cycle that begins in play, is formalized in organized games, and is nurtured by fantasy. Although I still can't get back past 1955, I can now playfully reconstruct how the process must have started. The Sportsworld gets its power through the gradual ritualization of each of the prior stages of development.

The Sportsworld consists of athletes, fans, coaches, managers, and executives; all are players. Howard Senzel's observations of baseball are true for the Sportsworld in general:

In this world of baseball the only legitimate activity is play. And so the only legitimate lifestyle is to be a player. And so, by emulation, proximity and desire, everyone who embraces baseball becomes, in some way, a baseball player.

Senzel recognizes that baseball consists of "commodity relations," but that it is simultaneously nurtured by illusion. Illusion, delusion, and play, as Erik Erikson has pointed out, all come from the Latin root word "ludere"—an indication of another connection between child's play and adult belief. Piaget has called play a "deliberate illusion." Senzel recognizes these connections in the following linkage of baseball with play: "To partake of shared illusion is the definition of play."

My concern is with how the Sportsworld emerges from the playing, dreaming, and imitation of children. The adult intensity of involvement is built upon this developmental process. The adult fan is linked symbolically to the athlete and his world precisely because of the biographical links to his own childhood play and fantasies. While it may be

74

possible to distinguish players from fans by definition, it is more fruitful to see both groups as connected by a symbolic canopy in the present as well as by shared historical tradition.

The fan is a spiritual athlete. The emotional link between the two is nurtured by the American view of the athlete as Peter Pan. Historically, the Sportsworld has encouraged the view of its athletes as innocent boys. The vigorous prosecution of those who might generate disillusionment (be spoilsports in the manner of the 1919 "Black Sox," for example) attests to the powerful pull of the symbolism of children at play.

The play imagery is captured in the biographical statements of contemporary athletes, which are important despite the trend toward debunking heroes. Bill Bradley captures this moment most eloquently:

In those moments on a basketball court I feel as a child and know as an adult. Experience rushes through my pores as if sucked by a strong vacuum. I feel the power of imagination and the sense of mystery and wonder I accepted in my childhood before my life hardened.

The fan immerses himself in the play symbolism. He reads the biographical statements, watches the dramatic and often joyous intensity of the game, and, at the same time, recollects and fantasizes about his own childhood triumphs, failures, and dreams. Irwin Shaw captures this in his *Voices of a Summer Day*. Middle-aged Benjamin Federov watches his son playing ball and reminisces about his own life, which is interwoven with the American game:

The sounds were the same through the years—the American sounds of summer, the tap of bat against ball, the cries of the infielders, the wooden plump of the balls into catchers' mitts, the umpires calling "Strike three and you're out." The generations circled the bases, the dust rose for forty years as runners slid in from third, dead boys hit doubles, famous men made errors at shortstop, forgotten friends tapped the clay from their spikes . . . coaches' voices warned across the decades, "Tag up, tag up!" on fly balls. The distant, mortal innings of boyhood and youth.

The memory of childhood play exerts a tremendous pull. As Kenneth Keniston notes, "For many adults, the immediacy and aesthetic depth of childhood experiences are never equalled later in life." Keniston also points out, underscoring the Peter Pan imagery, "The Holden Caulfields of this country love children because they love themselves best as children: it is the 'phony' grownups who are the objects of anger and pity." Robert Smith's comments about baseball are valid for all sports:

This I am sure is the lot of numberless American males, that they cling as long as life and common sense will let them to the days when a game of baseball could fill a whole hot afternoon so full that it would run over at the edges.

In their recollections, fans and players alike recall their dreams of glory and stardom. Alas, few will be able to realize those childhood dreams. Howard Senzel realized this early on. He made a pact with his friends that they would all never cease to rest until they became major leaguers; he worked religiously on his baseball fundamentals, but it was never to be. A fan was born: "What really interested me, even from my earliest memories, was *the world* of baseball." At this age, however, being a fan and remaining a player (despite the collapse of the dream) is quite common. Here the symbolism of the larger world penetrates everyday life:

76 Even out of the little games I played, bouncing a tennis ball against the back wall of our garage, I would spend the entire afternoon playing two major league teams, in a five game series. I would try to mimic each batter's actual style in the way I threw the tennis ball against the garage wall. It wasn't really baseball. And it wasn't really day-dreaming, it was metaphor.

Fairy tales and picture books are replaced by a larger mythology. The heroes of the Sportsworld permeate play and fantasy. As Julius Erving recalls:

Sometimes I'd go out on the court and shoot a ball and say somebody's name as though imitating their shot and their game, putting myself in their place, maybe hoping that one day I'd be out there.

Dave DeBusschere corroborates this: "As a kid you had a dream. Playing ball in Detroit Stadium where the Tigers play—I guess it was a fantasy. No, I think it was more a solid dream..."

The larger symbolism penetrates communication in everyday life as well. My cousin Jacob keeps the entire family in stitches doing his Luis Tiant imitation. While we were watching the World Series together, my son, Jonathan, grabbed a long Tinker Toy, bent into a low crouch, and yelled, "Look, Dad, this is Brian Doyle."

Heroic emulation is also a coin of peer group communication. Rick Telander, in *Heaven Is a Playground,* described the following sidewalk scenario in which a group of children are walking to school:

One group comes by and a boy runs out in front. He holds a candy wrapper in his hand and spinning around as though dribbling shouts, "Who am I?" "Earl the Pearl!" the boys cry. Then he holds the wrapper over his head and rotates his arms like a cowboy twirling a rope, before throwing the paper to the ground. "Who?" "The Doctor, Dr. J!"

Next he holds the wrapper gently in his palm and lofts a slow hook shot towards an imaginary basket no higher than his head.

"Jabbar! Jabbar!" the boys shout, jumping in the air."

77

Immersion in the Sportsworld's aura does not stop there. Newspapers bring children closer to their idols, and baseball cards often dominate the peer group activity. The cards become the basis for the discussion of the players' merits. The ability to memorize the statistics on the back becomes a source of prestige and acceptance. The holding of a personal icon smooths the way toward identification with the symbolic world. It is increasingly difficult to know where the Sportsworld begins and the world of everyday life ends. A child will frequently leave home with the ball game on his lips, his baseball cards in his pocket, his team jacket on his body, his Pro-Keds or Converse on his feet, and a baseball cap on his head.

As my own story illustrates, sports also has been one of the few areas where fathers and sons have been able to be close. Removed from the world of his father's work, the young boy may play catch with his father, watch the game with him on television, and occasionally make the longer excursion to the ball park. This involvement can have a tremendous impact on a youngster. Former Little League star Bill Masucci recalls:

But first I go back to when I was seven years old, maybe; my father used to take me on this train that ran from Schenectady to just outside Fenway Park in Boston. It cost him about five dollars a head... I loved it. My father and I...

Robert Smith captures the penetration of Sportsworld symbolism through the mediation of the father-son relationship in this reminiscence:

The major league park—it might be forty miles away—was the goal to head for on an overnight excursion, on which fathers could bring their sons to give them an early taste of the grownup world. One or two holidays of this sort every season would give a boy enough baseball to keep the flame of his devotion burning. For there were scores in the newspapers every day, usually on the front page, and stories of the game, pictures of the game's heroes to collect, a magazine devoted to baseball...

78

This father-son symbolism permeates the ethos of the Sportsworld and the larger culture. The father who sticks a bat and glove in his son's crib is a staple of American folklore, as are famous athletes whose success would never have been accomplished without Dad. Pete Maravich boasts that

Everything I know about basketball I learned from my father. I like to think that he made sort of a robot out of me, sort of a bionic person, because of what he wanted. I am not ashamed of that. He was instrumental in making me what I am today. Actually, you might say I was born with a basketball, because in early baby pictures I had one of the first basketballs made with the string tied to it, and my Daddy put it in the crib with me.

The Sportsworld comes to life for the child, and his own play is majestically enlarged, through the drama of the game. Youngsters witness the excitement of the drama at a very early age. As a pre-teen, Pat Smith, a former basketball player at Marquette, tells of being transfixed in a tree overlooking a famed Harlem playground:

The old Rucker Tournament was held in this park . . . When I was a kid I'd climb up into that tree. I'd stake out one of those branches early in the morning and I'd just sit up there all day . . . I was in a world of my own sitting up above the crowd and watching the great ones come and do their thing . . .

The drama fuels the youngster's emerging commitment. Smith describes with awe a confrontation between the late-arriving Connie Hawkins and Wilt Chamberlain:

The crowd was still hushed as they called time out . . . They surrounded the man. They undressed the man. And finally he finished lacing up his sneakers and walked out into the backcourt. He got the ball, picked up speed, and started his first move. Chamberlain came right out to stop him. The Hawk went up—he was still way out behind the foul line—and started floating towards the basket. Wilt, taller and stronger, stayed right with him, but then

79

the Hawk hook-dunked the ball right over Chamberlain. He *hook-dunked!* Nobody had ever done anything like that to Wilt. The crowd was so crazy that they had to stop the game for five minutes. And I almost fell out of the tree.

That kind of moment gets replayed, rehashed, and re-lived—in court action, enthusiastic retelling, and in the dreams of the young.

The drama permeates the young player's own play but is further reinforced by the growth of team allegiances. This process, symbolically reenacting its larger world model, begins on the sandlots. As Robert Smith recalls:

That may have been what made baseball so exhilarating to all of us, for it took us outside of our slums and often immersed us so deep with the common cause that skin scrapes, strawberries, bloody noses. . . were of so little account that we sometimes never felt them until the out had been made or the run scored.

The team breaks down stubborn egocentricity and installs a shared vision in the young player. No wonder that George Herbert Mead built his model of socialization on the concept of the team. In recent years, sandlot team play has given way to organized copies of professional leagues in all major sports. These teams assume a great importance in a youngster's life. An ex-Little Leaguer recalls:

I was really lucky, I thought, making the team when I was eight; heck, most of the kids got cut, and they were really shaken, crying and all of that. I can even remember how they used to do things when they cut a kid; there were so many kids trying out, it was unbelievable. But they never told the kids, "Hey, you made the team," or "Hey, you didn't make the team." They would tell everyone to look in the newspapers; they said that the kids who made it would have their names in the paper. . . Finally, the day came when the team rosters were announced in the paper; hey, I saw my name, and I went crazy—it was like Christmas.

80

The Little League team often is enhanced by the presence of a local minor league professional club, much more important before the advent of television. Another ex-Little Leaguer explains:

Look, when I was a kid in Schenectady, my heroes were the Schenectady Blue Jays...I thought God played on the Blue Jays...one night I caught a foul ball—hey, I was hooked on the Blue Jays for life.

The little leagues and minor leagues are just part of the team infrastructure. In many small towns the local high school is the foundation of the town's community identity. The importance of the team gets interwoven into the whole fabric of school and community life.

In their book, *Small Town in Mass Society,* Arthur Vidich and Joseph Bensman remark on how towns maintain an ideology of community toward reality when the real thing collapses. In small towns throughout the country, sports team partisanship is the bulwark of this ideology. In Massillon, Ohio, the high school team even has its own historian. The following description of high school football games in Texas underscores the point: "They are props for something bigger, something which is discussed in churches, bars...cafés, schools, Kiwanis club meetings, oil fields and out on the north forty. Football, particularly high school football, is the staff of life."

A major league team can have an equal impact on a youngster. Roger Kahn recalls his feeling about the old Brooklyn Dodgers: "They might even have been gods, for these seemed like true Olympians to a boy who wanted to become a man and sensed it was an exalted and manly thing to catch a ball with one hand..." Later on, Kahn became a reporter covering those same Dodgers and in one small remark captures the fantasy of involvement that is generated

81

in the process of socialization: "I strode out onto the plane, monarch of my dream . . ."

Playing on the team, watching the team, and dreaming about playing on the team are all intertwined. This synthesis is most clearly captured by Arnold Beisser's psychiatric profile of a young adolescent named Benny. Benny's family moved from St. Louis to Los Angeles and the move precipitated a schizophrenic reaction—estrangement, loneliness, and depersonalization. Benny was lost in the urban sprawl of Los Angeles. Gradually, however, he developed a rooting interest in the Dodgers. His therapy started to go better, the city began to take on a certain order—with the Los Angeles Coliseum as the center. "One day when the crowd rose to cheer a game-winning run, Benny realized that he too had risen and was cheering. This was an event of great significance."

The last key feature of Sportsworld symbolism that penetrates into the world of the growing fan-child is the image of authority. The penetration of authority often begins with the father, who initiates the youngster's interest in the world. The father quickly gives way to (or merges with) the coach. In the recollections of the Schenectady Little League champions of 1954, the figure of manager Mike Maietta looms large. Bill Masucci describes it this way: "I'm a success in life and I owe it all to three people: my father, Mike Maietta and Bucky Freeman, my coach at Ithaca. They taught me how to win, not only in baseball but in life."

The coach has tremendous impact. Chuck Neidel, conjuring up images of Plato's philosopher king, illustrates this impact: "Now Mike took each and every one of us and sculpted us into players. It was like, here he was with fourteen little pieces of clay, he chiseled away here and he chiseled away there, and when he was done he had created fourteen players." Besides influencing the youngsters on the team the Little League coach becomes a respected man in the community and is a visible symbol of authority.

Now Martin Ralbovsky doesn't like Little League coaches. He finds them dictatorial, immature, and frustrated individuals who exploit their players. By and large, however, the data from his own *Destiny's Darlings* question his own conclusions. With a few exceptions and not without a bit of hedging, those young men grown old recall the profound, positive influences that the perhaps frustrated, certainly dictatorial, Mike Maietta had on them.

The often dictatorial nature of the team set-up is generally perceived, by many black and working-class kids especially, as a place to gain acceptance, win respect, and learn discipline and a code of honor. Dave Meggyesy, certainly no knee-jerk admirer of Sportsworld clichés, recalls that he would "do anything" for Coach Vogt: "I was a real hustling fanatic once I stepped onto the football field. This was the first time I had ever received praise directly for anything I had done and I thrived on it." Meggyesy, escaping from a brutal father, turned to a harsh but disciplined coach, "and in a pattern I was to see repeated time and time again, the coach became a sort of substitute father. Vogt at times seemed to show a genuine concern, perhaps because he too had been poor and made it through college with the help of a football scholarship."

The high school coach as a personal authority figure has a profound personal and symbolic influence. Psychologist Daniel Offer found the coach to be the most respected authority figure in a school he studied: "As far as the students are concerned the athletic coaches are almost the only teachers in the high school environment who treat them as individuals. The coaches often serve as confidants, helping the students to overcome emotional hurdles." When school

83

sports dominate a community, the coach is also the most important man in town.

It is not that Ralbovsky is wrong and all coaches are the ideal fathers we always longed for. It's just that he misses how the authoritarian attitude is integrated within a world of meaning for the youngster who is often searching for direction. Nowhere is this more true than in the ghetto where fathers are often unknown or absent. A white Rick Telander was coaching a team of black youngsters against black coach George Murden, and he commented:

I watched George Murden's style—berating his players, pushing them on, demanding silence, obedience—his eyes always carrying the threat of violence . . . And it bothers me that as his players work and sweat and succeed they fill up with pride, the angry furrows disappear and they become a unit, molded from common suffering.

In the ghetto the coach is often the first adult male to approximate a father figure. For example, coach Gene Smith gave the young Connie Hawkins his first sense of self-respect, and Coach Fisher of Boy's High gave young Connie his first view of a white man who cares. Bill Russell eloquently expresses the essence of a coach's personal impact:

I was terrible, but Powles had faith in me as a person and didn't want to break my spirit. He had only fifteen uniforms for the team but carried sixteen players. I was the sixteenth and I split the uniform with a boy named Roland Cambell. By that one gesture, I believe that that saved me from becoming a juvenile delinquent. If I hadn't had basketball, all of my energies and frustrations would surely have been turned in some other direction.

All the aspects of the symbolic sports drama—the heroism, the team, the dramatic confrontation of the game, and the personal authority of coaches—penetrate into and emerge from child's play. They are nurtured on fantasy and dreams

84

and given reality in a developing network of social communication.

Harry Edwards has observed that the "sports creed" or belief-system derives from the "business creed" of the larger society and is conveyed through aggressive masculinity. Boys learn to be aggressive and to develop initiative and industry. At the same time, they learn to control feelings that might betray a vulnerability in the competitive struggle. Breaking down emotionally is quitting and the Sportsworld maxim admonishes, "Winners never quit and quitters never win." Other maxims reflecting this are "When the going gets tough, the tough get going"; "It's not the size of the dog in the fight, its the size of the fight in the dog"; and "Kill the weak and punish the strong."

The Code is learned from the biographers, the newspaper accounts, and through the actual playing. It is also learned from involved fathers and is passed on in the inspirational literature. Mickey Mantle tells of a time, early in his career, when he felt like giving up. His father's intervention was crucial:

I guess I was like a little boy, and I wanted him to comfort me.

He said, "How are things going?"

I said, "Awful. The Yankees sent me down to learn not to strike out, but now I can't even hit."

He said, "That's so?"

I said, "I'm not good enough to play in the major leagues. . . I'll never make it. I think I'll quit and go home with you."

I guess I wanted him to say, "Oh, don't be silly, you're just in a little slump, you'll be all right, you're great." But he just looked at me for a second and then in a quiet voice that cut me in two he said, "Well, Mick, if that's all the guts you have I think you better quit. . ."

Of course Mickey, as in all the other "true stories of heroism and bravery," is shamed into returning to the fray

85

and eventually triumphs, as do all the others who "have heart." The message is Horatio Alger's with healthy doses of Ben Franklin and Ralph Waldo Emerson. The lesson is clear: develop the appropriate character, and you will rise in this world. Bill Bradley's comments on Willis Reed underscore the message: "People underestimated his skill and determination... Willis lived by the aphorisms of his high school and college coaches who said, 'There is no harm in failing. Just pick yourself up and get back in the race'... 'A man's reach should exceed his grasp.' "

One of "Destiny's Darlings" emphasizes that he heard the message: "I learned one thing about life from that experience: nothing is impossible if you work hard to get it, that's been my theory for the rest of my life." The role of the coach often is instrumental: "If you broke down and cried in practice, he [Coach Maietta] figured that you'd break down and cry in a game. I don't think it hurt me a bit because that's what life is all about anyway, pressure and competition."

Mobility is especially important in the biographies of athletes of color or those from immigrant backgrounds. Yogi Berra's rise is seen as a "fantastic rags-to-riches saga," "an American success story."

Miracles happen in big league baseball. Take Yogi Berra for example. The son of poor immigrant parents, Yogi grew up on The Hill, a tough Italian section of St. Louis. His boyhood dream was to be a professional baseball player. His father, a bricklayer, was scornful of such youthful ambition. He wanted Yogi to become a laborer, so he could make good money.

86 We smile at the naiveté of the immigrant parent and a typical pattern unfolds. The immigrant parent is too locked into the old folkways; it is the second generation that socializes its parents as it is socialized itself. Stan Musial's Polish father was violently opposed to Stan's playing children's games. Joe DiMaggio's father wanted him to

follow in his footsteps and become a fisherman. This dual-level socialization is captured in a touching dedication in Roger Kahn's *A Season in the Sun: "For Olga Kahn,* student, litterateur, teacher, who at length is learning, in her eighth decade, which base is second."

Character, mobility, and Americanism all merge in the exposure to Sportsworld's imagery. Philip Roth attests to the power of the symbolism for the young fan:

To sing the National Anthem in school, even during the worst of the war years, generally left me cold... Nothing stirred within, strident as we might be—in the end just another school exercise. But on Sundays out at Ruppert Stadium... waiting for the Newark Bears to take on the enemy from across the marshes, the hated Jersey City Giants (within our church the schisms are profound), it would have seemed to me an emotional thrill foresaken if we had not risen to our feet (my father, my brother and me—together with our inimical countrymen, Newark's Irishmen, Germans, Italians, Poles, and out in the Africa of the bleachers, Newark's Negroes) to celebrate the America that had given to this disparate collection of *men and boys* a game so grand and beautiful.

The microsphere of the Sportsworld becomes an arena for personality adjustments as well. As Connie Hawkins explains, "Until I got good at basketball... there was nothing about me that I liked. There wasn't a thing that I could be proud of... It didn't seem like I had anything going for me..."

Connie slept long hours, appeared listless when awake, and was constantly beaten and ridiculed by the neighborhood boys. His brother Fred called him a "faggot." Gradually, however, his basketball skills increased and "the level of his 'game' became his measure as a man."

Being good at sports or merely being interested and knowledgeable facilitates social acceptance. The playground stars are known throughout a city's neighborhoods. The athletes are the most visible and popular boys in the school.

87

This process is underscored by a sign in Greenfield, Indiana, that once said: "Welcome to Greenfield, Indiana, home of Mike Edwards." Edwards at the time was still in high school.

The discussion of the socialization function of sports would be incomplete without illustrating the way in which the athlete has become a barker at a commodity carnival. "Reggie Bars" and "Pro-Keds" posters proliferate. Adidas and Puma T-shirts are a staple for the young players and fans. It is also hard for the young fan not to notice how Bjorn Borg resembles a walking billboard with his Bancroft racquet, his Fila shirts, his SAS patch, his Tuborg headband, and his Treetorn sneakers. If youngsters happen to get temporary blindness, the popular magazines offer stories, complete with the pictures of opulent living, on the new idols of consumption.

It is interesting to note how the new commercialized egotism is integrated—deliberately at times—within the old moral infrastructure. Just when the moneychangers threaten to take over the temple, some greedy soul falls flat on his face or some store-bought team collapses in dissension. The writers then drag out the old moral parables of team play and humility. Joe Morgan's comments are representative here. Once when asked about his value for the team, Morgan just shook his head.

No single player—not even a league MVP—should ever forget that he has to blend his own individual skills with the other 25 guys on the club as well as with the coaches and managers. Show me a so-called superstar who is selfish and doesn't fit in, and I'll show you a team that won't win the pennant.

Earlier I pointed out how play, games, and fantasy are interwoven. This takes on an added significance when we examine the role of sports fiction in socialization and escape. The role of sports fiction, falling somewhere between fairy tale and myth, has a relationship to "reality" that is truly unique.

The fairy tale is quite unrealistic. It functions as a screen for the child's unconscious feelings and anxieties. The fairy tale, as a struggle between good and evil, plumbs the darker side of human nature. The child identifies with the hero, usually an ordinary figure from everyday life. The identification with the hero, along with the emotional distancing that accompanies the form, helps the child externalize his or her crippling fears. The happy ending of the tales gives the child hope that he or she too, initially powerless and afraid, will be able to overcome adversity in the real world by following the hero's examples.

In myth, however, the hero is a superhuman figure who should be directly emulated. The fairy tale is a modest form and this prevents even the meekest child from feeling inferior and compelled. The mythic hero, on the other hand, always points up our own shortcomings.

Sports fiction is a combination of the fairy tale and the myth. At the same time, however, it has a different relationship to the child's world and to the larger adult world. This can best be explained historically. The use of sports fiction had a tremendous impact on the growth of the Sportsworld itself. Tristram Coffin explains:

Ralph Garber once wrote an article in the *English Journal* on the subject of baseball literature. In it he made the following remark about Ralph Henry Barbour, an early hack writer of baseball stories . . . "His clear and vivid accounts of the games in his novels were so superior to newspaper accounts of actual games that the sports reporting became more interesting as his books swept the country, *and the accounts formed the model for the reporting of real ones.*"

The symbolism of the sports drama was built on fictional sagas written for children. The Frank Merriwell stories had an even greater impact; the "Golden Age" of sports reporting

89

in the 1920s was replete with "Merriwellisms." The mythic infrastructure of Sportsworld discourse was taken from the fictional plots. Significantly, the same dramatic situations, plots, and resolutions are repeated in the sports reporting and journalism of today. The level of mythical discourse is certainly complex, and the historical linkage creates a universe of discourse with an unparalleled tradition in American life.

Frank Merriwell was a hero who had one of the greatest impacts on the imaginations of American boys. He was read by Babe Ruth, Woodrow Wilson, Jack Dempsey, and Wendell Willkie. The impact of Merriwell can best be gauged by the recollections of my father. While I was reading one of the Merriwell reprints, he came over to where I was sitting and proceeded to rattle off every leading character in the book and, in an amazing demonstration, summarized the plot—sixty years after he had read it! When I asked my uncle about Merriwell, he replied, "You know, I have never smoked because Frank Merriwell said it wasn't good for you."

Merriwell represented moral virtue. In the words of his creator, Gilbert Patten, "Frank Merriwell . . . stood for truth, faith, justice, triumph of right . . . [p]atriotism, sacrifice, retribution and the strength of soul as well as body." Merriwell helped translate the ethical ideals of Franklin and Emerson into the athletic code. His brand of hard-boiled practicality combined "rugged experience," "self-reliance," "perseverance," "self-assertiveness," and competitiveness with an ideology of fair play.

However unreal Merriwell was, he became the ideal in action of what every American boy wanted to become, "simply because the American way of life led him to believe the mythical accomplishments of Frank Merriwell possible." Merriwell displayed at the same time a type of masculinity that fit in with the athletic code and the business ethos. Boys who take a beating "well" are admired, and only the most outrageous insult could ever get Frank to show emotion.

Frank's control of emotions, his asceticism, and his triumph through struggle became a model for the capitalist "idols of production." Emerson's ideals of inner resourcefulness expressed through action, supported in the Merriwell fictional sagas, permeated the ideology of the economic world as well as influenced the coaching philosophy of organized sports. Significantly, it did so within a framework of Americanization and democratization. The plots are peopled by country boys, Swedes, Poles, and Italians. The leading villain in the beginning of the series, Bartley Hodge, is described as "well-to-do" and "foppish." Through exposure to Frank's example, however, young Hodge loses his class snobbery and spoiled demeanor to become "one of the boys," a defender of fair play.

While it was promoting rugged Americanism, the Merriwell series, like all fiction, offered young boys an escape as well. This is especially highlighted by Merriwell's own creator, Gilbert Patten—a repressed youngster and frustrated athlete. Frank was Patten's own escape hatch but, then "of course, the accounts reflect the basic frustrations of most lives, and obviously the reader as well as the author sees himself in the 'Merriwell role.' Men like Merriwell are everyone's dream of himself—secure, resourceful, capable...cool under fire...respected."

At the same time that the Merriwell stories were offering young boys an escape from the world, they were encouraging the belief that the Sportsworld was a clean and moral place and a refuge from the evils that beset the real world. When Bart, who wants to smoke and gamble, asks Frank, "Can't a guy have a little fun?" Frank replies, "Sure, but there are two kinds. One is wholesome, invigorating and good for building character, like baseball and football for instance. The other is spell-binding, injurio , degrading, like gambling." The fictional escape paved the way for the growth of the Sportsworld as a world apart.

John Tunis takes over from Patten as the next great writer of juvenile sports fiction. Tunis's books, more than Patten's, develop fully the entire symbolism of a maturing Sportsworld. The plots link city and country. *The Kid from Tomkinsville* comes out of a small New England town to make good in the threatening city; *The Keystone Kids* play in Nashville; *High Pockets* comes from North Carolina; and the *Iron Duke* comes all the way from Iowa to Harvard.

Tunis builds on the same moral infrastructure as Patten. These books were "object lessons." Tunis states in a preface that "all the characters in this book were drawn from real life." As Howard Senzel remarks, they were one step away from John Calvin, and "that authentic moral quality makes them more than just baseball books for boys." Senzel illustrates their influence on the Sportsworld in this way:

I read my John Tunis books during the same afternoons that I went to all the Red Wing games. And it was as difficult to separate them from each other as it is to trace any aspect of identity to a single influence. But the Tunis novels were the easiest and most convenient physical objects to attach symbolism to.

In all the Tunis books the hero faces numerous setbacks, is counseled never to quit, and eventually triumphs through sheer perseverance. Predictably the parallels between sports, life, and America are vividly drawn. Here Dave the old pro counsels the Kid: "You know, I've seen a lot of ballplayers, lots that had everything except courage. . . They just didn't have it and they couldn't work." A little later Dave remarks: "And baseball is all life, that's why it gets under your skin."

Tunis details the drama, the ascetic sacrifice, and the centrality of victory but adds another ingredient. Merriwell was written before the Age of Organization. Tunis, mirroring the changes in American political and economic life, emphasizes teamwork and personal authority. What is striking about the Merriwell stories is the singular absence of significant adults. Merriwell and his chums are the "band of brothers," the adolescents who built America without an older generation to rely on. The leading Tunis characters are youngsters who venture into the city and are molded into a team by concerned authority figures.

It is interesting to watch the way Tunis weaves the old moral infrastructure within a framework of team cooperation. Belonging is emphasized: "He was one of them, one of the gang, not an outsider anymore, but part of the machine...he had become part of the secret fraternity known as a baseball club." Class differences are not tolerated:

Perhaps we can't win the pennant. But there's one thing we can be, a team that's pulling together...[And there's] something else, too. That every man's as good as everyone...no matter who he is and where he comes from...

The fight against egotism (and capitalism) is seen within the framework of a larger citizenship:

You know, you're out there risking that throwing arm of yours 'cause you're one of them. You don't hesitate. You go out and take chances for the team...That's the trouble with this country nowadays, everyone's out for himself, aiming to hit the long ball over the fence.

Once the team becomes a unit the lesson is even clearer:

For now they were a team . . . thin and not so thin, tall and short, strong and not so strong, solemn and excitable, Calvinist and Covenanter, Catholic and Lutheran, Puritan and Jew, these were the elements that, fighting and jarring at first, then slowly mixing and blending, refining, made up a team, made up America.

93

The solidarity is reinforced by warm *and* forceful authority figures. Invariably a fiery Billy Martin or Leo Durocher type of manager is replaced by a Bob Lemon, someone warmly paternal. Tunis emphasizes how important the role of the manager is. The team's morale is collapsing until the strong conciliator steps in. In *The Kid from Tomkinsville,* a quiet Dave Leonard replaces a combative Gabby Street. And, while it is clear that Tunis sees a place for both managerial types, he prefers the one who treats everyone as individuals:

Different managers; different ways of running a ballclub. Gabby stressed fight. Fight and discipline. You had to do what Gabby said and like it. Every member of the club had to be in his room at eleven. . . Dave abolished this. . . Each man was to live sensibly, to do his own thinking on the field.

Interestingly, while Tunis is developing all these moral overtones he is slowly introducing the idea of the athlete as a financial symbol and an idol of consumption. (No, it didn't begin with Joe Namath.) In *World Series,* the Kid is getting jittery because "two or three thousand dollars are at stake. . . All that dough, more than he had made for his two seasons in the majors, on one game alone. . . Who knows: maybe he would make good after all? Might be able to buy a blue sports coat with blue striped pants and white shoes. And a big car with the top rolled back. . ."

The Tunis novels offer a wonderful chance to escape as well. Besides the basic rags-to-riches drama and David-Goliath confrontations, Tunis offers the warmth and camaraderie of the team as a refuge. The Kid watches the veterans in the hotel: "While he sat silently in a big chair, men kept coming downstairs, greeting old friends, calling in delight as they found a pal, laughing and talking, perfectly at ease with no worries and fears." The Kid, of course, is eventually accepted into this warm refuge. The same is true for the egotistical "Highpockets" McDade, who learns the importance of the team and is greeted *at home* after his game-winning hit: "He felt their bodies jostling his, the friendly contact of hips and thighs when he came across the plate, their hot paws extended to him . . . Now he was one of them, now he was part of the team."

These traditional themes are upheld by more contemporary writers such as Clair Bee in his Chip Hilton series, Wilfred McCormick in his Bronc Burnett series, and in the stories of Matt Christopher. As is the case with Tunis's work, the Merriwell themes are united within a framework of coopera-tion and acceptance. The centrality of personal authority and warmth is especially clear in Chip Hilton's sagas.

Chip Sr., a famous athlete in his own right, has died and left Chip's mother alone to raise the boy. Coach Rockwell, vividly symbolic as the tough but fair coach, becomes Chip's father-surrogate. This becomes especially clear in *Champion-ship Ball*. In the beginning we find that Chip has violated the coach's orders. He is, however, able to "unburden his feelings" and tell Rock how sorry he is. Chip is relieved by the coach's friendly manner and we learn how "all his uncertainty vanished." "I know how you feel, Chip," the coach said, "exactly how you feel . . . What say we forget about it . . . ?" Chip's confidence soars from this warm encouragement: "Suddenly he felt sure of himself."

The coach is a moral leader and sports is analogous to life. The coach as a paternal substitute is melodramatically illustrated later on in the book. Rockwell writes a letter to Chip's mom to assuage her fears about her son's mental condition. He tells her he is aware of it and is dealing with it. Next, "He glanced thoughtfully around the office and then walked over to the picture of 'Big Chip' Hilton which hung on the wall. Looking up at the picture, he muttered, 'He's a good kid, Old Timer.' " All's well, Mom and Dad. The coach is in charge.

The courts, playgrounds, fields, and arenas—set apart as they are—facilitate the feeling of escape. In a vivid pictorial essay entitled "The Dawn of the Possible Dream," *Sports Illustrated* captures the symbolism of the court-escape. The first picture silhouettes two boys on a court, lunging for a rebound in the approaching darkness in Venice, California. The next picture shows a black youngster watching, mesmerized, as his shot swishes clearly through the nets of a basket in a New York City playground. Another picture shows a boy dribbling down a dirt road in Newport, Rhode Island. The caption tells a brief but important story:

He is Walt Frazier or Jerry West, the future pro. But more than that, just lunging for a loose ball can be a marvelous act of desire, done over fallen leaves or on a court cleared of snow or in the summer when the city sizzles. A fast break is a boy's passion, and it is his training for the years ahead.

Growing up and being socialized into a complex society creates severe tensions, which are magnified by the child's own terrifying inner fears. The playground, arena, and stadium provide a place to escape these tensions. Julius Erving relates that "if certain things troubled me or there was a conflict at home, I would take my ball, go out to the park and play by myself for a few hours and it would make the whole situation pass by. I wouldn't be uptight anymore. I would really cool me out. . . It was utopia."

The feelings that build up and are denied any acceptable outlet can be discharged as a spectator as well. Howard Senzel shows how: "As I grow closer and closer to the core of my childhood alienation a shiver begins to run up my neck. Everybody needs to feel and I was no different. But when the feelings got too strong, too crazy, too morally ambiguous, or just too much to take, I had an alternative." And, further on: "The emotional content of baseball was wrapped up in my denial of feelings. Baseball was the escape from feelings.

96

Baseball was my relief from how I felt and how my environment demanded that I act. There is no place more important in life than your hideout, and baseball was my hideout."

Sports involvement—with a world of emotion, drama, and heroism—contrasts with everyday life, and can begin to dominate it. Sports can easily become the only reality for a person, especially during those hours at the ball park when a man can return to childhood and actually *be* that shortshop ranging over second base to stab a ball headed for the outfield.

The adult fan's escape is horizontal and vertical—into the game and into his own past. As Roger Angell notes while watching a game being played, "Sixty years have gone by, yet Napoleon Lajoie is in plain view and the ball still floats over to Terry Turner."

More important, the nature of sports as a male refuge must be further clarified. Until very recently, the world of political and social institutions was exclusively male. In order to be successful in these worlds men were trained, in good Merriwell fashion, to control their emotions, and to strategically channel them into accepted areas—preferably away from public life.

The Sportsworld of fact and fiction gives men and boys the one area where they can exhibit emotion and affection for their male peers. This is exhibited on and off the field, in the stands where men slap palms and embrace and in the locker rooms where towels are snapped and buttocks pinched. Connected with this is the way in which fathers and sons interact. Players and fans alike attest to the importance of Dad in their sports careers. 97

The male bonds and father-son connection coexist with the harsher reality of these interactions in the larger world. Keniston illustrates how the father is largely emotionally absent in the middle-class home, where the mother rules supreme. The *physically* absent father is a staple of literature dealing with the ghetto. And even in working-class homes, where the father is present, his presence is often threateningly unpredictable. In all cases, the Sportsworld offers a place for warm male communication that is absent elsewhere. This is why the fatherless Chip Hilton/paternal Coach Rockwell symbolism has had such a powerful appeal for young people.

Young people growing up can't quite get a handle on the roles the adult society has to offer. A major problem is the absence of any world view or "shared vision." The Sportsworld is, however, "an island of directness in the world of circumspection." Step by step from the playworld to the Sportsworld the child concretely enacts and internalizes the shared vision of the player. The athletic beliefs, roles, and institutions have a clarity unmatched anywhere else. It is a clarity forged in the euphoria of play and drama. The rituals of everyday life are passed from father to son to a clearly ordered future.

Unlike the rest of the society, where ritual bonds are absent, the Sportsworld, as a "seasonal masculinity rite," gives young boys at least one clear connection to adulthood. As my own story illustrates, it is the one important area where an adolescent can test his identity and masculinity.

The sports escape hatch is not only lateral into the game and vertical into one's own biographical past. It links the biographical with the historical past of the nation. A coherent sense of identity, besides requiring a connection with significant others, needs historical continuity as well. A major American problem, brought about by mobility and change, has been historical dislocation, which has contributed to identity problems.

The historical continuity of sports is a bedrock for American identities. This is best illustrated through the socialization of first-generation Americans. Silvia Tennenbaum's recollections illustrate the foundation of identity:

98

Baseball is a reflection of the American dream. Baseball is a mirror, held up to something profound in our lives—it gives us back our youth, our hopes, all our summers before the fall.

In my own case it also represents my initiation into American life; it was my rite of passage from being a German refugee, a kid with pigtails and funny clothes who couldn't speak the language, to being an American who rooted for the Dodgers and knew the difference between the bullpen and the catbird seat . . . and knew the crack-voiced cry: "Wait'll next year!"

Sports memories intersect lives and institutions. They evoke the past while they are symbolically reenacted in the present. They are, at the same time, as collective as they are intimate. They are the intellectual's passport to acceptance and the hard hat's vehicle for instant recognition of expertise. They are the heart of the American reality.

5. "Where Have You Gone, Joe DiMaggio?": The Political Implications of Sports Heroism

"For three years he had daydreamed of how he would be a scintillating high school baseball star and how he would hit a homerun with the bases full. And look at the way he had folded up in a pinch. Yes, after kidding himself about his destiny, and having the nerve to think that he would be a star like Ty Cobb or Eddie Collins, he was a miserable failure . . . He didn't have what it takes. He was eighteen years old and he was no good. He lacked something—nerve, confidence . . . Yes, even though he was considered one of the best athletes in school, he was never really going to be any good."

James Farrell, *Father and Son*

"In a good theatrical performance (as in ardent worship) actor and audience feel, 'We do it together.' "

Otto Fenichal

WHEN I WAS eight, the most significant figure in my life outside my immediate family was Mickey Mantle. When "the Mick" came to the plate my little body would tense up, a knot would settle in my stomach, and I would nervously pace the floor. I knew that with one swing of the bat Mickey could bring either joy or despair. This one human being held the fate of my team and my own well-being in his powerful hands.

Mickey Mantle as well as the lesser heroes of those great Yankee teams of the 1950s brought me into the warm confines of the sports drama. The outside world was confusing as well as foreboding, but the Yankee world made great sense. Mickey Mantle, Yogi Berra, Phil Rizzuto, Gil Mc-Dougald, and Whitey Ford provided me with an entry into a world of excitement and meaning.

101

The athlete is the human focal point of the sports drama. The following anecdote is a useful illustration:

On the final Sunday of the 1966 season, Sandy Koufax won the second game of a doubleheader in Philadelphia and with it a hot pennant race for the Dodgers. This was the last game he ever pitched in Philly, and it ended after dark. As the fans hurried across the floodlit field, two professors from the University of Pennsylvania stopped near the mound where moments before Koufax was struggling to triumph. One of them toed the slab and looking up at the obscure stands remarked, "If I had that guy's left arm, damned if I'd be teaching economics."

The part the athlete plays in the sports drama rests on the larger structure of the Sportsworld itself, which establishes its own boundaries in order to condense the human drama into the structure of one game, a pennant race, a play-off, a World Series, or a season. Neil Offen correctly points out how this condensation is "hyperlife under glass."

Drama does not exist without crisis, which rests on the possibility of meaningful human intervention. The background assumption of the sports drama is the existence of an alternative to a world in which human beings don't seem to matter. Destiny is in human hands from the commissioners' offices to the owners', general managers' and coaches' decisions. Dow Jones Averages, anonymous memoranda, and bureaucratic inertia are absent. Koufax faces Mantle with two on, two out; O. J. Simpson confronts "Mean Joe" Greene at the line of scrimmage; "Dr. J." swoops in on Kareem Abdul-Jabbar in the fourth quarter. Crisis and individual intervention are givens. As Mel Allen points out:

To a considerable number of us the sports world serves as the most accessible contemporary stage on which men of courage, boldness and determination can be watched! The issues are defined, the performances properly identified and the whole story immediately made available to the public.

The sports drama originates in the descriptions of the sportswriters whose purpose is to search for and underscore the dramatic crisis.

Hyperbole and publicity intensify the nature of the dramatic encounter, but the symbolism of the game itself provides the crisis atmosphere. The central aim of sports—victory—creates tremendous pressure, which becomes even more intense when the athlete represents his team and community. Losing is seen as sinful, akin to death. Losers are failures, the objects of our frustrations, pity, and scorn.

The crisis of winning is the emotional backdrop for hero-worship. Any threat to moral and community values produces tremendous individual and social insecurity. The athlete is the fan's life raft in this situation. His courage disposes of the threat of humiliation and chaos, and symbolizes the possibility of human control. The ability to assign "responsibility" to play along with human actors in a symbolically shared struggle enacted right before our eyes is the foundation of Sportsworld drama.

The pressure that emerges from the clear-cut alternatives of winning and losing is enhanced by the nature of a game as a mass ritual. Thousands of spectators chant noisily, obviously either loving or hating the individuals and/or teams involved. The tension and pressure on audience and actor alike enhance the emotional impact of the performance. Hockey player Eric Nesterenko gives us this atmosphere:

The pro game is a kind of stage. People can see who we are. Our personalities come through our bodies. It's exciting. I can remember games with twenty thousand people and the place going crazy with sound and action and color. The enormous energy the crowd produces all coming in on the ice, all focusing in on you. It's pretty hard to resist that [laughs] . . . These people were turned on by us [sighs]. We came off, three feet off the ice . . .

The dramatic pressure fuses the actor and his audience. As Robert Smith points out, people experienced a physical thrill when Babe Ruth hit a key home run: "What deep roars would

103

go up then! It was as if each person in the park shared with Babe the consummate release . . ." This dramatic fusion is generated by all the gifted soloists of sports. A description of Julius Erving highlights this general process:

Then, all of a sudden, the Sixers sprang to life . . . On offense, the Sixers fed Julius again and again and each time he made some impossible crazed, spinning, driving leaps toward the basket. It was pure magic and Philadelphia fans went nuts. This was no longer basketball but a kind of religious exercise with Erving as shaman.

The great athletes are charismatic performers who exude an emotional force that energizes those who bear witness. Writer-fan Woody Allen captures the fan's feelings in his description of Earl Monroe:

What makes Monroe different is the indescribable heat of genius that burns deep inside him. Some kind of diabolical intensity comes across his face when he has the ball. One is suddenly transported to a more primitive place. The audience gets high with anticipation of some great thrill about to occur . . . It's amazing, because the audience's "high" originates inside Monroe and seems to emerge over his exterior. He creates a sense of danger in the arena and yet has enough wit and style to bring off funny ideas when he wants to.

The star athlete imprints his personality on the game, the team, the fans, and, as often as not, the whole nation. The hothouse method of nurturing a sports star in a continual crisis atmosphere results in a process of ruthless selection. Those who survive to become the focus of an entire nation tend to have "stronger personalities." They don't crack under pressure, and in the terms of a classic sports cliché, they "want the ball in the last two minutes."

104

The importance of personality emerged during the 1920s, an era of personal publicity and glorification of the individual skills of athletes. This focus had, and continues to have, two important aspects. On the one hand, the fan *observes* and the reporters glorify the color and style of the performers during the contest. On the other hand, the media endlessly speculate about and analyze the inner workings of the star's personality. The twin-edged approach facilitates the entire process of identification. The fate of our athletes is our own. It feels "like a personal friend is out there fighting for us."

Each athlete develops an on-the-field manner and appearance that makes him immediately identifiable. The late Thurman Munson's neck gyrations, Joe Namath's slouch and white shoes, Kareem Abdul-Jabbar's sky hook all are commented upon and copied (where possible) inside the arena and out. The colorful performances and personalities ingratiate audiences and stylistically urge emulation and vicarious identification with all aspects of the athletes' lives.

The dramatic focus of the Sportsworld pushes the sports star into the role of symbolic leader, a model whose image reflects the values of the world in which he acts. The athlete's typing resonates with basic values of the "social system" of sports. The moral injunctions "hustle," "a winner never quits, a quitter never wins," "don't be a sore loser," "be humble," be a "team player" all generate the social types. Players whose on- or off-the-court behavior flouts the moral beliefs become targets for fan anger. The tantrums of Rick Barry invite audience hostility. The "cool" of a Walt Frazier is ridiculed as indifferent loafing. A nonhustling Dick Allen is an easy mark for abuse. On the other hand, those who grandiosely exemplify the normative structure are lionized. Pete Rose becomes "Charlie Hustle," Jerry West becomes "Mr. Clutch," and O. J. Simpson is lauded for his willingness to subjugate his ego into the larger good of the team.

The athlete is expected to perform with a grace and an understated flamboyance. The hero is always threatening to "become too big for his britches." There is always the danger he will think he is "bigger than the game." This is why such pressure is placed on the athlete to be humble and acknowledge his debt to his team or his sport. Even the immortal Babe

105

Ruth was censured for acting in direct disregard of the rules of his sport. As then-commissioner Kenesaw Mountain Landis remarked when he forbade Ruth's postseason barnstorming, "Who does that big monkey think he is?" We live vicariously in the ability of the hero to transcend all the pointless routines of everyday life. Yet we secretly rejoice when he is forced to atone for overstepping the bounds of that transcendence. In both instances the social order is reinforced.

It is no accident, then, that those athletes who are most despised are the spoilsports and the braggarts such as highjumper Dwight Stones and tennis player Jimmy Connors. Yet these villains are allowed to continue to play as long as their impudence does not threaten the world's order. In basketball, for instance, a rough enforcer is both feared and admired as he "subtly" keeps order on the court. If, however, his tactics lead to brawling and brutality—or, as with Kermit Washington, near death—the rules themselves are threatened and the athlete is ritually sacrificed. These rules are even more seriously invoked when games are fixed. The "dumpers" are sacrificed to preserve the game's integrity.

The dramatic appeal of the sports star is also linked to the ability of the Sportsworld to symbolically re-create the joy, playfulness, and spontaneity of childhood. This is one of the primary reasons why fans idolize the enthusiastic athlete. "Say Hey" Willie Mays, Mark "The Bird" Fidrych, and "Magic" Johnson transmit a joyful energy while playing. As players become more businesslike in their rhetoric we should look for even greater media emphasis on the joyful, playful "anachronisms."

106

It is important to point out in this respect that the enthusiasm of playing (performance) is linked to the seriousness of craftsmanship (ability achieved through years of hard practice). While it is clear that the athlete is "playing," the fan realizes through his own involvement that a lot of hard work lies behind the execution of a perfect shot. Every fan who has shaken his head in awe over a passing volley, a stutter step in the open field, or a "dipsy-do" lay-up understands this. Billie Jean King's discussion of the "perfect shot" illustrates this point:

The perfect shot. It's just an "aahhh"—all those years of preparation, the moments of losing and mis-hitting the ball, all those nights as a kid when I stayed out when the sun was going down . . . My heart pounds, my eyes get damp, and my ears feel like they're wiggling, but it's also just totally peaceful. It's almost like having an orgasm—it's exactly like that.

The synthesis of play, intense emotion, craftsmanship, and hubris is what permits athletes to regard themselves as great artists. Billie Jean King once again explains this idea:

When I'm in that kind of a state . . . I feel that tennis is an art form that is capable of moving the players and the audience—at least a knowledgeable audience—in almost sensual ways . . . When I'm performing at my absolute best, I think that some of the euphoria I feel must be transmitted to the audience . . .

The athlete helps instill important values. Wiley Umphlett notes that "heroes represent a people, and by discovering the meaning of their character, by returning to the roots of their behavior, we discern the moral figure in the tapestry of the nation."

The sports star, as a "vernacular hero," moves with the ebb and flow of everyday life. We can learn a great deal about the values that are taking hold within ordinary lives and mass consciousness by looking at who rises as an athletic hero at a particular time.

107

Sports, particularly baseball, became an important national phenomenon as American society began to modernize and industrialize. The growth of railroads and the telegraph enabled local "townball" teams to begin to venture out and compete against each other. The assembling of youth from all over the North during the Civil War allowed the "New York game" to be taken back to all areas of the country. Baseball (and to a slightly lesser extent boxing) information and talk began developing as a communicative bond among various sections of the country. The stars were the vehicles of identification: "Baseball had its national heroes worshipped by small boys from Maine to California. There was not an American who did not recognize the name of 'Pop Anson,' 'Iron Man' Joe McGinnity and Honus Wagner . . ."

A star would become famous locally and then move onto the national stage as his skill and reputation swelled. When John L. Sullivan won a big fight, Boston would turn out en masse to welcome him home. When he was defeated, by James Corbett, "the world seemed to totter. An incredulous public refused to believe the dire news that appeared in bold-faced headlines from coast to coast." Coffin condenses the relationship of baseball and national communication in this way:

After the Civil War, when baseball was formulating, America needed a national game, as well as national heroes, legends and literature, to shore up its pride, soothe its self-consciousness, and explain its attitudes . . .

Baseball was quickly equated with Americanism. It also exhibited a dual-edged appearance that later characterized the Sportsworld as a whole. Baseball was emotionally perceived as an "escape" from the evils of urban-capitalist life. The scenic backdrops of the ball parks—their dirt and grassy fields—encouraged the feeling that the game was an idyllic pastoral refuge. Yet the parks' cramped surroundings in narrow urban lots and their billboards emphasized that the escape occurred only within urban-capitalist borders. Whatever the scene, however, the values of the sport resonated sharply with those of the developing capitalist system. Mark Twain recognized this when he wrote that "baseball is the very symbol . . . the outward and visible expression of the

108

drive and push and rush and struggle of the raging, teeming 19th century."

The competitive values of sports were tied into the Horatio Alger myth of mobility. The symbolic value of seeing people rise from lower origins through sheer skill and determination cannot be underestimated. Robert Smith points this out in his baseball history:

As the New England town meeting, by habituating the colonists to democracy, doomed the manor system, baseball, by setting no other standards than craft and skill and brutal determination, helped get the common people into the habit of honoring a winner without regard for his antecedents . . .

The democratization process was linked with political and economic factors. The game itself, originally an aristocratic stronghold that restricted the participation of common people, began to recruit players from all class backgrounds as gambling interests pushed out "etiquette" in favor of the ability to win with any methods available. The polite, no-sliding, "don't take advantage" game was replaced by the more ruthless (*"ungentlemanly"*) tactics of people like John McGraw and "Pop" Anson. This change reflected the increased competitiveness of the economic order.

As baseball was nationalizing the democracy, it was proving to be an excellent vehicle for the difficult task of Americanizing the immigrants. The immigrants needed to be assimilated into all the newly emerging cultural values—values that were by no means secure even among the native born. Threats to conform always fluctuated with more palatable forms of inducement. As sports grew more acceptable, they became a symbol of the immigrants' embrace of the American system and the openness and receptiveness of the system itself.

The immigrants' mobility drama was certainly not limited to baseball. Boxing heroes evolved with each new influx of

109

ethnic groups. The growth of football at the turn of the century exhibited the same trend:

The ethnic significance of football is immediately suggested by the shift in the typical origin of the players' names on the All-American football teams since 1889. In 1889, all but one of the names (Hefflinger) suggested Anglo-Saxon origins . . . By 1927, names like Casey, Kipke, Oesterbann, Koppisch, Garbisch, and Friedman were appearing in the All-American lists . . .

Notre Dame, with its Irish and Polish gridiron stars, became the symbolic embodiment of ethnic American success—especially when it overtook the Anglo-Saxon Ivy League in football supremacy.

The ethos of democratic competition permeated the Sportsworld belief system. An important aspect of this creed was the notion that participation in sports could help potential delinquents caught in the squalor of urban ghettos. Educators such as Richard Ely and G. Stanley Hall felt that sports built good "character." The "Y" movement, the Boys' Clubs, and the Knights of Columbus all picked up this theme and institutionalized the idea.

People in the settlement house movement such as Jane Addams marveled at the way sports gripped the mass consciousness and sought to use this enthusiasm to achieve their own ends. This thrust at the grass-roots level paralleled the growing media portrayal of the athlete as an innocent. Christy Mathewson truly was a clean-cut "YMCA type" and not really typical of the average ballplayer. "Yet there was a tendency in those days to accentuate, to exaggerate or even invent a pure and gentle side to every human endeavor. Mathewson was treated not as an unusual figure, but as a typical figure . . . The periodical writers undertook to dress the game . . . in clean rompers at every opportunity." And, as Robert Smith points out, the glorifiers portrayed baseball as a crusade led by "clear-eyed scout masters."

110

The success of a capitalist society rests upon a legal-rational system of authority, and this need was reflected in sports. At the turn of the century, the structure of football rules was in flux and even those rules that were accepted gave rise to arguments over their improper enforcement. Gradually a stable body of rules evolved, along with methods to smoothly deal with necessary changes. Similar currents were visible in baseball. Administrators such as Ben Johnson sought to bolster fan faith in the rules by enhancing the dignity and professionalism of umpires. Periodic attempts to deal with the suspicion of bribery were also important ways to inspire faith in the rules.

Suspicion remained over the incorruptibility of baseball, however. After World War I, when baseball was booming, Chicago baseball writer Hugh Fullerton uncovered a major game-fixing scandal. Public furor mounted, far transcending the later dismay over President Harding and his cabinet. Swift and effective action was demanded. The hiring of a baseball "Judge Roy Bean"—Kenesaw Mountain Landis—proved to be the remedy. Acting quickly, overruling a jury that had acquitted the players who were accused of fixing World Series games, Landis banned the "Chicago Black Sox" for life. The Black Sox sins were ritualistically purged through banishment, and Landis became a true ethical hero of American life.

More important, however, Landis personified the integrity of the rules (as did the Black Sox through their victimization) and restored public confidence in the sanctity of the national pastime. As a result, sports entered its Golden Age and emerged as a national mass movement. All of this had tremendous significance for the role of sports as an agent of socialization.

111

Sports' role in socialization and the generation of political cohesion took a dramatic turn in the post–World War I period. The decade of the twenties saw America go "sports crazy." It is important to see how the growing sports phenomenon meshed with some significantly new political and social trends.

The 1920s marked a watershed in the development of American capitalism. During the turn-of-the-century period of industrialization, the thrust of socialization aimed at "proletarianization," the creation of an army of hardworking citizens. As American industry increased its industrial capacity, and as integration of the work force remained a problem, new policies were needed to neutralize industrial tension. This became crucial during 1919, a year of intense anti-capitalist political activity that provoked the repressive Red Scare. Obviously, inducements other than police raids were needed to head off militant workers.

The rigid subordination of worker to the factory, characteristic of Frederick Taylor's "scientific management" movement, gave way to more subtle yet more thorough attempts to integrate workers not only within the factory but beyond. Enlightened businessmen and the growing corps of human relations experts began to see the possibility of creating "citizens of industrial civilization."

It is no accident that the postwar period also saw the simultaneous eruption of a national sports movement. The nationalization of sports was crucial to the entire movement toward consumption and political and social integration. The role of athletic "heroism" was a key factor in both the rise of sports and the larger processes of socialization. The Golden Age was an age of personality and flamboyance that fueled all the postwar trends. It was Babe Ruth who propelled the game of baseball out of a period (1919–1921) when the threat of radicalism and inflation was causing great anxiety. Robert Smith has observed:

Yet despite all these alarms, there seemed always men and boys enough to crowd a baseball park. And when Babe Ruth appeared

112

there were usually so many fans ready to put strikes, international disputes and the high cost of living out of their minds that the bleachers could not hold them.

The heroes of the Golden Age quickly extinguished unpleasant political memories. The business of sports itself took on a heroic quality. Promoter Tex Rickard lifted the sport of boxing out of a quagmire of moral suspicion through the force of his flamboyant personality and his keen insight into the need to promote the essentially dramatic nature of the match. Rickard carefully groomed his heroes and his villains and spent lavishly to give boxing an aura of respectability.

This period's sportswriters explained the phenomenal growth of sports in terms of dominant personalities: "Never before, nor since, have so many transcendent performers arisen contemporaneously in almost every endeavor of competitive athletics as graced the 1920s."

The heroic deeds became the language of national communication. Paul Gallico's remarks on Dempsey are prototypical: "But nearly everyone in every walk of life seemed to love and admire Jack Dempsey. There was hardly any class to whose imagination he did not appeal . . ." Dempsey's national appeal was probably transcended by Babe Ruth's:

Ruth incognito was a contradiction in terms. Even in that era before television and mass circulation picture magazines . . . everyone knew and recognized Ruth's huge round, flat-nosed face . . . wherever he went Babe was on public display and few, if any, of his peccadillos went unnoticed.

The creation of national heroes dovetailed with the movement toward the nationalization of a consumer culture. The athletic heroes symbolized the new era of consumption. As the ad men were promulgating the idea that "freedom" and "democracy" inevitably involved the consumption of goods, athletes were personifying the idea in their own symbolic dramas of success. The "Babe" truly was a symbol of the age;

113

his salary disputes were good copy and it was always clear what he needed the money for: "Aside from the esthetic appreciation of his own worth, Ruth needed more money because he was spending more and more of it—on clothes, on automobiles, on girls, on partying . . ."

The athletic heroes not only were idols of consumption, but examples of social mobility. Paul Gallico's *Farewell to Sport* has a chapter on Gene Tunney entitled "Horatio Alger, Jr.," that eloquently captures the symbolism involved in the rise of a bank clerk (his B.A. from Yale was downplayed) into the upper echelons of society:

No fictional story ever based on the beloved rags to riches theme was ever more unbelievably fantastic or more characteristic of the cockeyed post-war sports period that made it possible. Twenty-five years ago it could not have happened. It took war, post-war inflation, an unprecedented sports mania . . . and Gene Tunney himself, probably the most remarkable of all the people who were featured in the success story to end all success stories.

In boxing if often didn't matter if one did not fight well. The excitement of seeing poor, struggling, often immigrant young men earning hundreds of thousands of dollars in a few moments was enough of a stimulus. The "up-from-poverty theme" was dramatized by the intense focus of the media on the lives and personalities of the athletes. When Ruth seemed to break all the normal human limits of eating, drinking, spending, and fornicating, outrage was always muted by the popular knowledge of his "orphan" beginnings. That "half-brutes" like Dempsey and Ruth from "across the tracks" (as were most Americans) could become rich beyond maddest fantasy fueled the popular imagination, mobilized the instincts (to consume), and reinforced a faith in the larger political and social system. As Gallico says, "It is one of the favorite fables of our democracy, and when it comes to life as it sometimes does in

114

startling places, we are inclined to regard the lucky character as more royal then royalty."

The consumption by athletic heroes fit well with the growing political ideology of consumption, which sought to equate the consumption of goods with political freedom. "Democracy" resonated with the proliferation of consumer choices and by buying people legitimized a growing cultural apparatus of control in the name of individual liberation. The ability of the athlete to symbolize an "escape" from the routines of everyday life—Dempsey's ability to "lick any man in the house," Ruth's tendency to act like a spoiled child— effectively mobilized people for consumption.

The thrust of the consumption ideology was aimed at creating individual insecurity. Products were pushed as compensation for personal inadequacy. Ads made people "emotionally uneasy." In fact, the growing consumption ideology offered people an escape from the very ills capitalism itself had created. If the process of rationalization turned people into isolated, anxious cogs in an industrial machine, consumption offered the possibility of escape by offering "mass-produced visions of individualism by which people could extricate themselves from the masses." The "triumph of mass idols" offered the "spectacle of an outstanding life" that was securely rooted in the evolving capitalist system.

The 1920s marked the initial phase of the development of an ideology of consumption. It was not, however, until after World War II that consumption could be effectively internalized and practiced by a larger majority of Americans. The intervening depression was an era of retrenchment as the advertisers waited for a better day:

115

Beyond the realm of goods, media were mobilized to sell what could be bought: a spirit of fraternity and commitment, a sense of justice within a vigorously conserved sense of order. The popular arts and cinema enjoyed a heyday. The radio became an integral tool of politics and culture. These combined to generate an ideology of raw frontier idealism and moral commitment, an idealism of acceptable scarcity, resilient cultural fiber, social realism, hard work and fortitude.

In this climate, the "Gas House Gang," baseball's St. Louis Cardinals, flourished—a team of fibrous, never-say-die ruggedness. Baseball salaries were cut and sports stars reenacted the old pre-Ruthian verities. The symbol of the age was boxing's James Braddock:

He was a unique product of a specific era . . . Braddock ascended to the title in the waning years of the depression, having fallen from an earlier prosperity and then pulled himself out of the poverty and despair with which so many of his countrymen were only too familiar. "The Cinderella Man," they called him, and perhaps no other champion had been so real a national symbol.

This shift in the content of heroic models demonstrates how the Sportsworld resonates with shifts in the socioeconomic and political climate. It acts as a separate symbol system yet moves within the boundaries set by the larger culture. The shift in sports symbolism is in response to the change in people's needs caused by a changing reality. Sports symbolism then moves to alleviate hierarchical tensions: "Braddock inspired an unprecedented wave of public sympathy and good will. The millions whose spirits and imaginations had been stifled by the depression clutched at Braddock as a symbol."

An extensive analysis of popular biographies, sports magazines, and the daily paper demonstrates that today's sports heroes, with adjustment for more modern packaging techniques, are perfected and expanded versions of the consumption idols of the 1920s. Interestingly enough, many of the earliest themes of Americanization, "sanitization," and mobility are still present, acting as important bolsters to the larger ethos of consumption.

Many people object to the designation "hero" for today's athlete. Fans and commentators often take issue with the publicized "immorality" of athletes and the media examination of all the stars' personality flaws. The objections go like this: "No matter how sophisticated our youth have become, they are still young and need someone to emulate. They need the Gary Cooper portrayal of Lou Gehrig. . .In this age of complicated personalities, an idol without known faults and deficiences is necessary."

Heroism need not emerge from rigidly set down ethical guidelines, though. The hero-model moves with whatever is culturally significant at a given time. The commercialization of the sports star naturally spins off from the development of a consumer ideology. This is especially true when the world of commodities itself increasingly replaces any normative basis of legitimacy for the political system as a whole. What is heroic, then, is what contributes to the common good of buying and selling. This is reflected in the Sportsworld through the use of different types of athletic heroes for the encouragement of consumption.

The linchpin of this process is athletic performance. From that basis many kinds of personality images are used to promote popular consumption. Joe "The Stud" Namath is pitted against Fran "The Boy Scout" Tarkenton. Yet when we turn on the television, Namath and Tarkenton are earnestly peddling the products the advertising people feel are representative of the groups each athlete symbolizes. Each symbolic model provides a way into tapping Sportsworld energies for the corporate system.

The turmoil of the 1960s saw the breakdown of consensus in American society. The rise of sports heroes with divergent appeals reflected this breakdown. Who one rooted for began to be determined by the athlete's political views and life-style. The politicization of athletics added to the possibilities for hero worship and villainy. The controversy ultimately, however, was rooted within the commodity structure. Dick Young's fulminations against Joe Namath brought a "Thank God for Dick Young" from Namath's business manager,

Jimmy Walsh, who quickly realized the controversy merely enhanced Namath's market value.

The politicized athletic controversy was indeed a profitable drama. Robert Lipsyte's mordant pen captures this in discussing the complementary roles of Namath and Vince Lombardi:

The two men complemented each other, Lombardi was football's frontman, while it was promoting itself as a sado-masochistic weekly adventure show written by Robert Ardrey, Konrad Lorenz and Lionel Tiger. By mid-decade, when territoriality and male bonding were slipping, Joe Namath arrived with that outrageous price tag on his arm. By the end of the sixties, Lombardi was firmly established as the Father and Namath the Son while football was being packaged and sold as psychodrama . . .

Generally, however, Namath and his heirs were the vanguard of a radical hedonism that began to take root in American culture. What we have here is the democratization of Ruthian excessiveness. Increasingly, what Americans could only do vicariously through heroes like the Babe became possibilities for their own lives. Namath's impact resulted from his ability to stylize rebellion. He was able to symbolize the antiestablishment values of youth while inducing an acceptance of the larger commodity structure. He transformed the counterculture into the "over-the-counter culture." Larry Merchant captures this subtle synthesis:

Namath drove a Lincoln, lived in a penthouse, was a devout hedonist . . . and would rather go one on one with Dick Butkus than sit in the mud for three days at Woodstock and listen to rock music. But America saw him as a hippie and there was no doubt in anyone's mind that if he were a girl he wouldn't wear a brassiere . . .

The "Namath Effect" ushered in the era of Rolls-Royces, penthouses, llama rugs, fancy wardrobes, and stunning "female accessories." The Reggie Jacksons, Ken Stablers,

118

Walt Fraziers, and Frank Tananas are style leaders for an era of free living intricately connected with consumer ostentation. The media preoccupation with salaries, more and more a staple of Sportsworld communication, is linked in article after article with a consumption-based ideology of "freedom," "fun," and "individualism." This reference to tennis star Vitas Gerulaitis is typical: "Gerulaitis, who has flowing blond locks and a vast array of high fashion clothes and high class ladies, loves his gaudy bachelor life style. You only live once, he says, and you better smell the roses while you can."

The athlete is also a leading symbolic advance man for the sexual revolution. As a persuasive representative for the hip promiscuity of our times, the athlete is a trend-setter for the fluid relationships that increasingly characterize our society. We must be prepared to easily pick up roots and move on. Gregariousness and quick and easy intimacy fit this trend. Sexual promiscuity contributes to political and social integration; the cheap availability of sexual release creates an illusion of freedom. Increasingly, however, this freedom acts as a "garland chain" to anchor individuals more securely in the routines of the established order.

Sexuality and its integrative functions are increasingly portrayed by athletic models in the media game of kiss-and-tell. Joe Namath tells us, "I can't imagine anyone who doesn't enjoy sex, who doesn't want sex all the time. It's the best thing ever invented." Marv Fleming lets us know that "Women made my career." The opposite sex ratifies the notion in stories about female "groupies" like Linda Huey's "I Gravitate toward Jocks."

It is important to emphasize that heroic symbolism is not so completely one-sided. The sybarites and swinging singles are counterbalanced by solid family men, clean-living kids, and working-class heroes. Thus we hear about Tommy John: "John does not resemble your everyday athlete. He is articulate, literate and quick-witted. He wore a vested suit of

119

Oxford gray, tailored in Brooks Brothers style; a solid blue shirt; burgundy tie and new shoes. His hair was neatly styled." Later, after learning of his All-American upbringing, we read about how his devoted wife helped him recuperate from an injury that nearly ended his career: "For months his arm was useless. He had to be fed and clothed by his wife . . . Doctors thought he would never pitch again. He exercised his hands with rubber bands and Silly Putty. Within months he and Sally, who had just recovered from the birth of their first child, were working out in the yard of their home in Yorba Linda, Calif. He lobbed pitches that she caught with a softball mitt."

We also learn about the simple life of Larry Bird: "He doesn't care about material things . . . He prefers denim to double-knits and traditional high topped canvas shoes to the sleek, striped leather models which know no bounds between stars and reserves nowadays." Bird initially turned down a multimillion-dollar pro contract because of his commitment to Indiana State University. Morality and the antimaterial spirit survived within the apparent breakdown of values in the larger society and eventually contribute to the ethics of excess in a slightly ironic end-around. The following year, when his professional options were greater and his image had more luster, Bird signed a professional contract for $650,000 per year for five years—the largest rookie contract ever. (Watch for Bird's Seven-Up commercial.)

Money erodes traditional norms—generating lavishness, ostentation, and envy—and creates the need to cut people down to size to preserve the normative structure. For some years now, Dick Young of the *Daily News* (typifying an important group of sportswriters) has done this job well. He has questioned the political radicalism of Bill Walton, attacked the "racism" of Kareem Abdul-Jabbar's black nationalism, and has turned almost visibly nauseous at the glorified permissiveness of Joe Namath and Reggie Jackson. His single

120

most important theme has been how money has eroded Sportsworld's values, bringing showboating, egotism, and arrogance in its wake. Ah, but money even penetrates the consistency of Dick Young's moral outrage. In a column on Pete Rose, he cannot hide his admiration for "clean living and dirty uniforms" being rewarded—to the tune of $700,000 a year: "He's unique, Pete Rose is. Not only on the field . . . He is a hard-hat millionaire, a deese, dem and dose guy who majors in double negatives . . . He may be ungrammatical, but when Pete Rose tells you something you can take it to the bank."

Young finally has a hero of his own, a throwback to another era who nonetheless receives the big bucks all the "jerks" are getting. The money factor becomes less important because someone with the "right character" has hit the jackpot.

The promotion of consumption does not eliminate the traditional Sportsworld mythology of hard work, mobility, and innocence. The "Rocky-like" stories of a "too small" and "too old" Vince Papali still harp on the theme of guts, determination, and effort—even though Papali is eventually cut from the team. We still hear how athletes such as Lyle Alzado, Ron LeFlore, and Mike O'Koren escape the hellish squalor of the big-city ghettos for the sanitized heaven of the Sportsworld. The "moral" infrastructure is, however, linked with the "amoral" but socially important push to consume. A work ethic is maintained within the commodified world of fun and leisure.

The athlete as actor and public persona symbolizes someone who has "got it all together." This is, of course, often linked to all his women, cars, and clothes. The credibility and vividness of the athlete's persona is illustrated by the deadness the ballplayer feels when his playing days are over. Ex-basketball player Jim Barnett explains it as "a tough period of my life. I know it doesn't look so tough . . . I have a nice house, and we just had a new baby . . . but you've got to measure that stuff against not playing . . . the adoration of the fans; the great pleasure of leading a fast break and scoring over a tall opponent; the big money . . . all of it over."

The "high" of the athletic performance is tough to give up. As Bill Bradley points out, "I've been preparing for the end since my first year, but even so I can only hope that I will manage easily the withdrawal from what Phil Jackson called 'my addiction.'" The popular accounts of the deathlike retirement of athletes underscore the youthful joy athletes symbolize in "their life." The prolonged joy of adolescence is over at age thirty-five. Listen to Mickey Mantle:

"I loved it," he says, his voice throbbing with intensity. "Nobody could have loved playing ball as much as me . . . I must have fifty scrapbooks. People sent 'em to me. Sometimes after breakfast when the boys go off to school, I sit by myself and take the scrapbook out and just turn the pages. The hair comes up on the back of my neck. I get goose bumps and I remember how it was and how I used to think it would always be that way."

The athlete's vivid public self is a "shared high" that compensates for the depersonalization of the larger society. Through what Orrin Klapp calls the "vicarious voyage of identity," fans can share the intensity of public recognition. Fred Exley grabs this moment in his discussion of his feeling for Frank Gifford:

I cheered for him with such inordinate enthusiasm, my earning became so involved with his desire to escape life's anonymity, that after a time he became my alterego . . . Each time I heard the roar of the crowd, it roared in my ears as much for me as for him; that roar was not only a promise of my fame, it was its unequivocal assurance.

The star athlete is like a cult—a shared experience in himself. Fans crowd around their favorites hoping to get an

122

autograph (talisman) or merely to just touch greatness. This phenomenon penetrates into everyday life in the consumption of news about one's favorite hero, the organization of fan clubs, and the interminable debate over "Who was better, Mantle or Mays?" that enlivens water cooler, locker room, and barroom discussions.

Sports heroism "solves" identity problems in another related way. It confronts the impersonal bureaucratic structure with a drama of individual accomplishment. The ideology of individual accomplishment and mobility is still important to the structure of American capitalism. As many have pointed out, however, this ideology is not now nor was it ever really congruent with the reality of a class society. During the earlier phase of industrialization, though, the Alger ethos fit more comfortably with American reality. With increased complexity and bureaucratization the gap between ideology and reality widens. This situation encourages *psychic* mobility. We all become Clark Kent or Walter Mitty.

Psychic mobility allows people to escape from the restrictions of everyday life, restrictions that contradict the exhortations of political and social mythology. This brings us back to the role of symbolic drama. Margaret Mead's comment is to the point: "The assumption that men were created equal, with the equal ability to make the effort and win an earthly reward, although denied every day by experience, is maintained every day by our folklore and our dreams." Once the myths fail to *approximate* reality, "social and personal tensions result."

American ideology holds the individual *responsible* for his own success or failure. Intense guilt, fear, and anxiety emerge from this situation. Rising levels of anxiety pose dangers for the maintenance of personal self-esteem. Karen Horney highlights the effects of competitiveness, linking the high incidence of neurosis to the larger forces at work within capitalist society.

123

Horney points out that "neurotic" competitiveness underlies the entire pursuit of power, prestige, and pleasure. Such "neurotic" competitiveness is used as a way to alleviate the anxious helplessness and insignificance engendered by the processes of the capitalist system. This competitiveness generates a heightened sensitivity to frustrated ambition. The existence of an ideology of competitive individualism creates a zero-sum game among people. "Who's on first" becomes a literal concern. Hostility and isolation are what emerge from this situation.

Competition isolates people from one another. As Bob Cousy indicates, you need the "killer instinct" in order to succeed: "On the court I had that instinct . . . I would climb over anything or anyone to succeed, whatever the cost to me or anyone else." But, the success of a Bob Cousy frequently is not available to the rest of us. Most of us don't have the limelight to compensate for our competitive isolation from others—our ambitions and our reality fail to coincide. This lack of congruence can become so unbearable that it demands a remedy, which often is a flight into fantasy.

Identification with athletic heroes offers the "illusions of intimacy." The guilt and risk personal relations often engender are eliminated in "para-social relationships." We can love them, share their experiences, learn their "innermost secrets" in "intimate relationships" without the risk of their disapproval. Their role demands that they put up with all our irksome adulation. The existence of a cult around the athlete enhances the illusion of intimacy as does the anonymous yet nonthreatening warmth of a filled stadium. We not only form para-social relationships with our athletic heroes, but we also participate with them on the field as they hug, kiss, and slap the palms of their teammates in the euphoria of the moment. Our isolation is alleviated through the identification with the symbolic drama of warm affection.

124

Frustrated ambition usually is displaced onto concrete individuals or groups within a social system. Identification with the sports hero works in two ways to allay the hostility that is often generated by frustrations. The sports star is often engaged in a good deal of controlled violence. Through his vicarious voyaging the fan gets the chance to relieve his pent-up anger. Paul Gallico captures the sports version of Clark Kent's transformation into Superman in his description of the "common man" appeals of prize fighters:

The most popular thing a sportswriter can say about a prize fighter, the good old standby, is that outside the ring you would never take him for a pug. No, sir, more like a bank clerk or a businessman. Just as quiet and gentle—loves birds and flowers, you ought to see him with his kiddies on his knee . . . But what Killers when aroused! Could that soft-spoken fellow with the well-cut clothes, the rather queer laugh, high-pitched voice and the perfect manners be the Jack Dempsey who clouted Jess Willard until he resembled nothing at all human? . . . How wonderful to be so quiet, so gentlemanly, and yet so terrible.

The sportswriters play on the averageness of the hero outside the arena. Ethical objections notwithstanding, this averageness aids in the fantasy dramatizations of ourselves that are enacted through identification. The desire to tell the boss to "take this job and shove it," the impulse to throttle the mugger instead of skulking away, the imagined thrill of depositing the loan shark in the incinerator are all played out in the violent dramas of sports:

125

If we could we would all be gentle, soft-spoken creatures, tender with women, cool and even tempered, but once aroused—"Whap!" A lightning like left or right to the jaw. Down goes truckdriver or hoodlums. We mentally dust our hands, readjust our cravat, smile pleasantly, step over the body of the prostrate victim, and carry on.

Averageness resonates with the democratic requirement that the hero must not rise too highly over the mass. He must be "one of us." His uniqueness is confined to the arena—outside he is just a more colorful version of the "Good Joe."

The drama of sports heroism functions so well as a receptacle for repressed emotions because of its ability to turn anxiety into stress. Anxiety is amorphous, free-floating, and immobilizing. Stress, on the other hand, arising out of a concrete, fear-producing situation, is easier to come to grips with.

The sports hero provides a dramatic glimpse at how sports function in American society. The sports hero, in all his evolving uniforms since the turn of the century, has been an important transmitter of dominant values.

The role of the sports hero has also been instrumental in the personal development of the individual. The sports stars are within the fantasy reach of millions of children, who learn the important cultural assumptions through heroic identification. Later on, however, as the cultural assumptions prove to be difficult to achieve, children and adults maintain their intense identification because it serves as a method of resolving anxiety that was generated by the overblown expectations in the first place. This channeling process, or fantasy release, helps reestablish an emotional equilibrium that allows the continued pursuit of the important values. Anxiety is stimulated and then put to political use. The individual, however, is continually caught in a vicious circle that prevents him from seeing how his personal distress is intimately connected with the political processes. Instead of being encouraged to confront this dilemma by powerfully working for political and social change, he is induced to flee his real self for a partial life among abstractions.

Sports involvement in this sense approaches the character

of a neurotic symptom, almost like an obsessional neurosis. As psychiatrist Henry Kellerman points out:

People who are fans keep rooting for the same things day in and day out . . . Each game they want the same thing to happen. That's because on a symbolic level they can't work anything out at all . . . If the conflict on a reality level remains in your life, then you can root for something symbolic over and over again. If the conflict is resolved in reality, you don't need to be a fan anymore. The symbolic isn't necessary for you to act out your needs. To put it another way, sports can be cathartic, but never therapeutic.

This giving-up process powerfully supports the ongoing political and social system. Frederick Exley's confessional admits as much:

In a moment I would fall asleep. But before I did, all the dread and dismay and foreboding I had been experiencing disappeared, were abruptly gone . . . I understood, and could not bear to understand, that it was my destiny—unlike that of my father, whose fate it was to hear the roar of the crowd—to sit in the stands with most men and acclaim others. It was my fate, my destiny, my end, to be a fan.

The ability to live in a symbolic life among abstractions is an abdication to those people who are able to concretely mold public policy for their own interests. The individual is incapacitated for the project of reconstructing his personal life, a reconstruction that is linked to the larger political and social institutions. People are rendered powerless insofar as they are unable to see the ways in which their personal concerns are related to the larger structure of society.

What's more, the isolation, hostility, and deception that characterize our age of rationalization and "impression management" is allowed to continue to poison our community life.

Franz Neumann has shown how an understanding of anxiety is critical to an understanding of politics. The focus of

127

politics, he tells us, is "the dialectical relation between freedom and domination." It should be clear that freedom entails an understanding of how the forces of domination act both outside and within the individuals of a society. Sports has always been portrayed as "above politics." This rhetorical subterfuge has allowed it to inculcate political values through a stylistic "end run." The "life-world" of sports offers a refuge from the entire structure of commodity capitalism at the same time that it acts as an important member of the consumption team.

In the role of fans we can participate in the thrilling "spectacle of change" while the powers that actively shape our society remain out of our control. The exhilaration we feel in the symbolic "breaking tackles" in our imaginary display of dazzling open-field running from the forces that restrict us seriously increases our risk of being "blind-sided."

6. Of Team Players and Sky Hooks: The Infiltration of Sports Language in Politics

"We have sort of an expansion ball club that's fighting in Vietnam at the present time. The South Vietnamese will not win every battle or encounter but they will do a very credible job."

Melvin Laird, former Secretary of Defense

E NTER A PITTSBURGH bar and listen. "Oh, man! Terry was cool! Three large studs ready to stomp his behind, and he just danced, spotted Lynn, and hit him right on the money! That's my man!" Walk past the playgrounds of New York City. "Oh, sweat! The Doc copped that pill in one hand, skied o'r top three dudes and threw that sucker down!"

Wherever there are sports fans, you will find the talk, the warm, lively retelling of yesterday's game, the playfully serious arguments over players' talents and umpires' calls. The boastful partisan predicting, "No *way* are those turkeys gonna beat us tomorrow." Games and players long since forgotten come back to life with astonishing vividness. Individual exploits take on the cosmic significance of a confrontation between gods.

The talk is not conversation in the usual sense. It is reenactment. Watch the wildly gesturing arms, the expert imitation of obscure movement, and the festive slapping of palms. In the same way that going to the game lifts us out of mundane reality, talking about the game and the players is itself a form of escape from nagging frustrations and dull routines. The Sportsworld comes to life in talk, and the talk brings life to everyday surroundings.

130

A few years ago, I went to dinner with a group of lawyers. A young Chicana lawyer was part of our party. All efforts at drawing her out into conversation failed; her replies were short and without emotion. The conversation shifted naturally to sports, and, without warning, the woman enthusiastically jumped in, explaining in animated tones her love for the De Paul University basketball team. She went on about Dave Corzine's moves, Gary Garland's shooting and the muscle work of Joe Ponsetto. Every detail was lovingly described. Just as suddenly, her mother lode obviously tapped out, she withdrew back under her cloak of timidity.

A recent *Sports Illustrated* survey found that 72 percent of all Americans saw themselves to some degree as sports fans. In sharp contrast, those who are knowledgeable and avidly follow the events of the political arena are part of a shrinking population. Because of this widening gulf between sports interest and political apathy, politicians and those who analyze politics increasingly have turned to sports language and sports metaphors in order to generate interest and communicate information about politics.

The rise of sports language and its subsequent use in political discussion says a great deal about the relationship between sports and politics in this country. An understanding of language helps to explain how the Sportsworld is able to create a dramatic power that performs important political and personal functions.

The political turmoil of the 1960s led to the growing politicization of athletics. At the same time, politics itself was being athleticized.

President Nixon frequently was photographed in some scene of sports significance. If he wasn't at the ball park or in the locker room, he was phoning the winning team and its coach to congratulate them. When political demonstrations against the Vietnam war engulfed the capital, the President pointedly watched a football game. Even more significantly, on the morning of the invasion of Cambodia, the President met with a group of protesters at the Lincoln Memorial. After

131

asking them what colleges they attended, he immediately began discussing their football teams.

This breeding of sports and politics is perhaps best exemplified by the increased use of sports language in political communication. Cabinet members are referred to as "team players." The invasion of a country is described as "Operation Linebacker," and the military commander is called the "head coach." Making a job easier for a colleague is referred to as "doing downfield blocking," and an ally that needs a great deal of political and military bolstering is referred to as "an expansion team." Politicians aren't the only people using these sports metaphors. Political commentators have borrowed this "sportugese" and by extension see politics in athletic images.

The proliferation of sporting usage to describe political actions and events indicates a significant relationship between the two worlds. In the first place, the use of sports analogies and the borrowing of actual sports settings point to the pervasive influence of athletics in American life. Red Smith grasps this when he indicates that "one measure of the stature of sports in the American scheme is the extent to which sporting terms are employed away from the playing fields."

It is through language and settings (or "scenes," in a dramatic sense) that we communicate common symbols. A distinct sports language indicates that the Sportsworld is a separate province of meaning. Language, communication, symbolism, and group life are inseparable pieces of a common plot.

The existence of a sports jargon demonstrates that sports fans are linked to a common perspective. The "world view" of sports is embodied in its scenes, slogans, and jargon. If this is true, then the use of "sportspeak" by political leaders and political commentators, as well as the posturing of politicians in front of sports backdrops such as ball fields and locker rooms, means the values and motives of sports have seeped

132

into the conceptualization and carrying out of political action. How this happens and the political consequences of its happening need to be explained.

The appeal of sports language cannot be grasped without first understanding the social context in which its appeal flourishes. We live in an increasingly rational and bureaucratic time that tends to create obstacles to effective communication. Unfulfilled needs for contact and communication rise accordingly.

The increased complexity of industrial society introduces the problem of creating and maintaining a comprehensive set of symbols for the entire society. Older, stable value systems become fragmented or completely erode in the face of industrialization. The problem isn't merely "getting an idea across" but effectively dramatizing a common purpose as well.

Language rests on an emotional and communal basis. It transfers basic emotions into symbolic imagery. As society becomes more complex, though, so does language. Yet as language becomes more scientific and abstract, it becomes less rich and no longer links people together. Style, beauty, and form become downgraded in the face of the "objective uses" of language.

With increased division of labor, each bureaucracy or social subarea develops its own specialized jargon. These scientific and technical vocabularies contain a very low emotional content. Ideally, they are suited for signaling bureaucratic movements, but they lack dramatic power.

The increased use of technical explanations and statistically laden speech deadens human interest. People lose interest in and attachment to the political and social orders once these orders lose the ability to persuade, to entice, and to dramatize a sense of allegiance for their mass audience. The political speech or the public service message is an inconve-

133

nient interruption from the more colorful appeals of sports, popular culture, or Dear Abby, for that matter.

The traditional political system and its language cannot convey a sense of human meaning. When there are no answers to the questions of why we are here and where we are going, the path has been cleared for the aggressive return of the mythical. An impersonal and abstract social and political system fails to provide the emotional feedback that human beings seem to thrive on.

Because the political world is bewildering, politics becomes the creature of the language used to describe it. Metaphors and myths are used to simplify the complex events that cause anxiety in people. In turn, the kinds of metaphors or vocabularies we use will inevitably structure the kind of reality we perceive and act on.

In order to make the political world closer, warmer, and more comprehensible, it is necessary to employ metaphors that will convey a warm sense of the familiar. Given a complex and impersonal environment, it is essential for political speech to tap areas where audiences do experience warmth, clarity, and personal satisfaction. Political metaphors can dramatically call forth new worlds in which remedies for personal distress are clearly perceived. This is best accomplished through an accepted vocabulary both speaker and audience understand.

Because politics is threatening, much political communication is repetitious, using a small number of classic themes that continually serve as explanations of political reality. Such repetition cues the listener that the world is moving along familiar routes. These classic expressions have the ability to keep conflict within comfortably circumscribed areas while at the same time closing off fresh insights.

The use of worn-out metaphors can just as easily reduce interest as reduce threat. In a political system with little conflict over basic values, dramatic appeals tend to become stale. Since our candidates tend to be relatively indistinguishable around key issues, alternative ways of generating political interest must be found. The remoteness and threatening impersonality of political action is overcome through the symbolism of entertainment and the arena. As one perceptive observer has noted:

Failing to organize our politics around politics, we organize it as entertainment; sometimes it is a horse race, sometimes an interminable TV sitcom. Hey—Jimmy Carter just picked up six delegates in Kansas . . . how about that, sports fans? Even our political literature is getting less political these days, tending ever more to dramatic, novelistic forms.

Glamour, personality, and the pure enthusiasm of the political contest turn politics into the consumption of dramatic images generally devoid of ideological content. Politics, no longer an arena for moral indignation, becomes part of popular culture: "Politics is to be appraised in terms of consumer preferences. Politicians are people—and the more glamorous the better. The manner and mood of doing things is quite as important as what is done."

Style and the aesthetic sensibilities of the discriminating shopper become the key ingredients of political success. With the mass media becoming the barker for a political carnival, glamour and gossip are used to combat indifference. Glamour is retailed; our political personalities take their places in the pantheon of *Us* and *People* magazines. Yet something is missing. Because the politics of entertainment or the entertainment of politics is inevitably a weak imitation of those areas where drama, conflict, and heroism exist in pure form, the values and appealing ways of more dramatic arenas begin to strut their stuff on the political stage.

Spectator politics must compete for the entertainment dollar and overcome its poor reputation among the voters.

135

The appeals of the Sportsworld, on the contrary, are already known and loved. As James Reston points out, "The world of sports has everything the world of politics lacks and longs for . . . They have more pageantry and even dignity than most mass occasions in American life; more teamwork, more unity, and more certainty at the end than most things . . ."

The Sportsworld has become the arena where grace, form, and ethical content still survive. It not only creates a seemingly autonomous world with its own ethical imperatives (slogans, morals, legal proscriptions), it also creates a powerful communal bond. The Sportsworld, with its ritual celebrations, its magical performers, and intense audiences, effectively counteracts the decline of emotional connections in the larger society. Arnold Beisser gives us a good illustration:

Everyone needs to feel he has ties with others. With the dispersal of the traditional extended family, the clan and the tribe, this need to be identified with a group of some kind has become more intense. The sports fan has a readily available group to satisfy this need, at least in part. He has a meeting place where he is needed to support the team. He can gather with others, don his Dodger cap or some other identification badge, and yell at the top of his lungs for his teams . . . In effect, by doing all this, he becomes a member of a larger, stronger family group, or collective entity comparable in some sense to the tribe or clan.

The communal bonds that are created in the festivity of the sports drama are sustained in language. "Sportspeak" is the glue that cements the activities of sports into a common emotional package. The rise of sports to its present level of mass involvement cannot be understood without an understanding of the historical evolution of sports language.

The rise of sports language can be traced to the development of the sports page around the turn of the century. The struggle of tabloids for a mass audience saw the development of yellow journalism, comics, and a separate section in the newspaper devoted solely to sports. The newspaper sought to widen—to democratize—its appeal and sports was a vehicle for such an appeal. This is still evident today. A great number of New York "sophisticates" (myself included) read the *Post* or the *Daily News* precisely because of their elaborate, colorful sports coverage.

Democratization slowly gave rise to a "national sports-consciousness" that was inevitably linked to a distinct dialect. As the sports historian John Betts has written:

With the rise of a national press and the popularization of sporting journalism, with millions playing organized games on the playground or the athletic field, with the development of a national sports-consciousness, enrichment of the American language is inevitable.

The sports dialect's democratic appeal was linked to its ability to reach people in a concrete, tangible, and emotional way. As sportswriter Marshall Hunt points out about Captain Patterson and the New York *Daily News:* "It was Patterson from the beginning who saw we would increase circulation by developing a strong sports department. He always wanted us to write in a bouncy way. Very biff, bang, boom stuff."

Style was extremely important in the appeal of the sports page. The 1920s, the "Golden Age of Sports," saw this style become distinct jargon. "Informality of style, originality of composition and a new jargon blossomed onto the sports page—but accompanied by a tendency toward verbosity, triteness and shopworn cliches, synonyms and analogies." It is precisely this use of jargon (overlaid with a stylistic originality) that makes sports language so appealing. Ritualistic language creates a predictable and understandable world of meaning, while at the same time condensing emotional responses. Sportswriting strives primarily to simplify and vivify. "It is clear that the selection of sports verbs and adjectives is not based solely on the objective content of the events . . . but also to convey part of the color and emotion of the contest . . ."

137

The effect of dramatic simplification is bolstered by the involved attitude of the reporters themselves. Unlike the political or economic reporters who are supposed to remain neutral, the sportswriter more often than not is an unabashed partisan. In Gallico's words: "I believed in it and was impressed by athletes and what I was seeing. And while the title of your book is *No Cheering in the Press Box,* I've seen and heard plenty of cheering in press boxes when we sports writers got excited by something."

The sports fan is not only emotionally involved but knowledgeable: "Spectatorship involves more than merely watching. It involves a great deal of cognitive ability on the part of spectators. It involves knowledge, an increasing knowledge. It involves expertise." The fans demand accurate information:

According to newspapermen . . . no class of readers is more responsive and none demands a higher degree of accuracy than the sports fan. The baseball writer especially is writing for an informed readership, and, if he makes a mistake, both he and his paper will get a dozen letters in the next morning's mail calling attention to that fact.

The development of a "national sports consciousness" and a distinct medium for its communication paved the way for extending sports symbolism into the political realm. So far, former President Nixon has been the most sophisticated in seeing the possibilities inherent in this extension. Nixon's use of the sports metaphor derived from his complete self-identification with the world of sports. His relatively non-Machiavellian preoccupation with sports has been observed by almost all those who have commented on the former President's sports involvement. After all, only a true fan would have gone—privately—to a Washington Senators' double-header in the 1950s.

As the focal point of the American political system, the President becomes the receptacle for much public expectation and fear. An effective device for identification in American politics has always been the image of "one of the boys." For Richard Nixon, as Gary Wills has underscored, the impression of being an average guy has always been important. Wills reports that Nixon had a genuine dislike of snobbery: "Football was always his way to remain 'common' during his triumphs on the long debating tours of his time." This desire explains the numerous (and politically effective) visits to locker rooms, phone calls to coaches, and receptions for sports figures. The use of sports terms and the "team" metaphor, as William Safire has observed, are useful because "they relate so closely to people." This fits in with the previously reported relationships between democratization and the rise of sports language. If the sports reporter is able to become part of the action he is conveying, and is able to develop a sense of empathy with his audience, it is not hard to envision a similar process between a political leader and a mass public. As a "symbolic leader," the President is for many people the personal link to the political system. Since sports does appear to many as a personal and concrete universe, the identification with its language and scenes is a way to develop a sense of the personal. The vicariousness of this relationship is part of the consumption pattern. It also encourages a sense of "false concreteness" about a complex and abstract political process.

Nixon's self-identification with the world of sports went beyond involvement with its ceremonies. He also seemed to believe that the values of the Sportsworld were those needed to "succeed" in real life. James David Barber and Gary Wills both indicate how Nixon's description of his "six crises" reflects the competitive "never-say-die" ethos of the athlete competitor. It is the ethic of Frank Merriwell and Horatio Alger:

It became fashionable in the years after Nixon's crushing defeat in 1962 to ask him what kept him running. It was the same thing that kept him on the football field where he did not belong—the sacredness of running, the need to deserve luck eventually by showing the pluck that starts at the bottom and never quits.

That simpler world of competitive "character" and success is anachronistic in the light of the past century's development. Yet it is a world that is preserved in all its symbolic clarity in the realm of sports. The transposition of that value system into a technocratic political system falsely clarifies the new complexity with the images of old simplicity. This is especially true since many of these values still continue to be accepted by many people.

The nature of sports language, warm and vital, emphasizing the concrete and personal at the expense of the abstract and logical, may prevent its users from being able to theorize and universalize. The use of sports language encourages sending complex messages through an oversimplified conceptual and syntactical framework. This inevitably leads to "noise"—but, significantly, "melodious noise."

Sports is a universe of controlled conflict. By using sports symbolism in political discourse the politician or commentator tends to transpose sports' ideologically unproblematic nature onto politics. This has the effect of underscoring the organizational (instrumental) imperatives at the expense of articulating substantive goals. It promotes an interest in who is "winning" or "losing" without looking at the reasons why one *should* win and the other *should* lose.

This tendency is evident in the use of such terms as "team player," "quarterback" (for leader), and "expansion team": The use of the team concept is an attempt to instill an "us-ness" where victory (which is morally unambiguous) is essential. If the South Vietnamese are an expansion team, for instance, they are first of all typically *American*. Second, what do you have to do with an expansion team? Everybody knows that such a squad must inevitably go through the "building" process of "stockpiling" talent. With the help of

140

the "expansion draft" we eagerly anticipate the rise of the South Vietnamese Rangers into a first division team.

Interest may be piqued and loyalty instilled but not without paying a heavy price. Domestically, a similar process occurs. If a political commentator tells us that "Senator Muskie has been placed in the line-up as a possible Democratic running mate," our attention is focused on whether "Ol' Ed" gets his licks rather than what's in "Ol' Ed's" head. (This, of course, overlooks the atrocious misapplication of this baseball term. If someone is "placed in the line-up," then, barring unforeseen circumstances, he should get his at-bats. Ironically, and almost certainly unintentionally, this "line-up" applies more to the process of picking out a criminal suspect for identification.)

The use of sports symbolism in political discourse is essentially a conservative device that prevents thinking about new policies and directions. Perhaps in order to move forward we must in some ways overcome *and* recover the past, but the Sportsworld is too often a place of refuge from the present. The attempt to transport its genuine apolitical and ahistorical appeals to our political and historical world will, further, make the political present more difficult to comprehend.

The rise of sports language and its subtle transposition to less dramatic arenas underscore the symbolic strength of the Sportsworld itself. Its use as a prop for a disinterested electorate offers neat insight into the evolving relationship between sports and politics. The strength of sports language and drama demonstrates how the symbolic world of sports provides for an emotional network in American society that forms an important foundation for political stability. The power of sports language, as an agent of sports symbolism, forms a network of national and social communication that provides large masses of Americans with communal warmth and personal identity. In such a role, sports language is the

141

glue for a diffuse "rain or shine" attachment to the American system.

Exactly. Carter's response demonstrates how the Sportsworld functions politically through its ability to work its way into the very marrow of our lives. Its richness provides a meaning for millions whose lives are impoverished by disenchantment with the larger society. The symbolic fullness of the Sportsworld highlights the deficiencies of the world that surrounds it. The Sportsworld's playground emerges from the squalor of its surroundings to offer people a spectacle of excellence, individual heroism, and identity. Yet street poet Jim Carroll's warning must always be heeded: "The playground is this world of total possibilities, but it's fenced in."

The challenge is to transform our society by opening up the fences and allowing the beauty of the playground to spill over and transform the world in the euphoria of play.

7. America's Team: Postgame Wrapup

"Without any winners we wouldn't have any goddamn civilization."

Woody Hayes

"It's not whether you win or lose but how you play the game."

Grantland Rice

A POSTGAME wrapup is customary in the Sportsworld; it weaves together the larger drama's subplots. It is ritualistically soothing as well as emotionally necessary because the excitement of the sports drama often leaves people drained and bewildered. The events need to be put into perspective, which the wrapup accomplishes by dissecting the past and anticipating the future. My own wrapup fulfills a similar purpose.

This book has demonstrated how the Sportsworld exists as a dramatic, symbolic universe that generates an emotional impact and creates meaning for millions of people. I have probed the way in which the symbolism of sports can produce intense personal devotion while simultaneously existing at the level of public celebration.

Nothing more dramatically underscores the impact of sports drama than the meteoric rise of the U.S. Olympic hockey team to the center of the national stage in the winter of 1980. A description of these dramatic ingredients underscores the workings of the Sportsworld.

The Olympians captured the American imagination through the essential crisis of confrontation that continually gives the sports drama its emotional meaning. The sportswriter as dramatist colored the clash in the traditionally appealing hues of David versus Goliath, or, in this case, by alluding to another seemingly invincible team of the mid-1970s:

This was the Big Red Machine that the American hockey team was playing. This was the greatest hockey team in the world. This was literary symbolism come to life. A hockey team emblematic of its army. A hockey team that rolls out human tanks and waves of troops in graceful assaults on ice to conquer any land . . .

The awesome Soviets are pointedly contrasted to the averageness of our own heroes. Compared to the assumed superiority of the Russians the American players are "rats" whose "scrapping play underlies their roots. . ." The American players are invariably described as "a bunch of college kids," "just a group of guys," "dead-end kids." Their humble beginnings, their amateur status underscore the unfolding drama of self-justification. As Bob Drury reports, "These guys think they deserve to skate on the same ice as the Russians. And if you listen long enough you begin to believe them."

The Canadians invented the game, the Czechs and Swedes played it well. But for three decades the hockey teams of the Soviet Union owned it . . . They came to the capitalist World and mopped the Madison Square Garden ice with the NHL All Stars . . . The statistics were enough to make Americans underdogs even if they substituted snorkel guns for hockey sticks.

The drama is built upon the personalities, histories, and symbols of the teams and players outside the arena. Only the game itself, though, can bring these themes to light in the intensity of the conflict. Slowly, as the U.S. and Russians remain undefeated, the climax draws near. Hope and trepidation are neatly combined in the tension of anticipation. Listen to the players:

Mark "Magic" Johnson: "They want the gold. Especially the way the politics are going. They'll be ready."

Mike Ramsey: "No team's invincible, but the Russians are close. If they have a weakness—and I don't know if anybody has found it yet—it's when you forecheck 'em . . ."

Mike Ramsey: "No one wants to go out and say we're gonna beat the Russians. But I'll tell you, if we stay close, get some goals early, pick 'em up much earlier, well, that's all there is to it."

The stage is set, the meaning of the game is clear, and the pressure mounts as game-time approaches. The game itself dramatizes the myths as it provides us with an outlet for catharsis. Chants of "USA!" "USA!" "USA!" reverberate throughout the Olympic stadium. People remain standing with intense anticipation. When Mike Eruzione scores what proves to be the winning goal, fans and players are locked in a euphoric embrace. The final minutes are tense as the clock slowly ticks off and goalie Jim Craig brushes away shot after shot. And then, "That's it! We won!" The players swarm Craig in an orgiastic spectacle. Fans likewise mimic the players as they hug one another in the stands. Flags appear from everywhere. "USA!" "USA!" "USA!"

The crowd, as Greek Chorus, joins the action and gives it meaning. The players are spiritually lifted by the cultic piety of the screaming congregation. Goalie Craig remembers: "I could feel them all game and especially in the last ten minutes. That had a lot to do with it." The euphoria spills over from the arena into the village of Lake Placid. One fan, part of a screaming, dancing mob in the village, shouted, "This is the greatest thing I have ever seen!"

The postgame symbolism is vivid:

They stood patiently on their own blue line with their chins on their sticks, twenty subsidized Merited Masters of Sport named Tertiak, Mikhalov and Krulov, watching a bunch of college kids throw their sticks, helmets and gloves at the ceiling and wrestle each other to the ice . . . And twenty heroes of Socialist Labor were standing all in a row waiting for a silver medal.

146   The pictures also tell the story. On front pages throughout the country on the morning of February 23, 1980, Americans were treated to photographs of a mass patriotic love-in. Even more delicious, however, was the wire service photo of three glum Soviet officials who provided a wonderful reminder of the meaning of the sports drama.

The game becomes a drama because of our identification with the team, which begins to develop a collective identity in striking contrast to the "upper-class" Soviets:

They are blue-collar athletes, the working-class heroes of the Winter Olympics. Their dirty blood-stained uniforms stand out amid the expensive ski attire and sequinned figure skating outfits.

The members of the U.S. Olympic hockey team are reminiscent of the 1950s "good boy" fraternity. They were rough and tough, drank beer, played practical jokes, and fought among themselves. Yet throughout all of this tumult a team given no chance emerged as a cohesive communal unit. These "salt of the earth kids" individually sacrificed and became "Team America."

The team's victory also symbolizes the emotional warmth of collective effort. Craig was nearly smothered by his teammates, but he loved it: "I couldn't breathe after a while, but, hey, I love these guys . . . They don't have to say it or sing it, but they *are* family."

The collective images and struggles of the team are personified by the leadership of coach Herb Brooks, who steadfastly refused to build the team on the star system. "We're a family, twenty guys working together," Brooks kept repeating.

In the Denver *Post* columnist Dick Conner drags out some of Brooks's quotes from the summer underlying how the present victory was the result of patience and hard work on the part of the team's leader. " 'Our long-term goal is to compete for medals,' Brooks said in the heat of July. Lord, how he looks like a prophet now in the ice of February." The team's joy of communion rests upon a foundation of hard work and sacrifice.

In the postgame analyses reporters continually underscore Brooks's inspirational leadership. For example, "Ah, coach Brooks was the most controversial personality on the team, if

147

not the entire Olympics. There's no question he earned himself a lot of gold last week. But his contribution to the triumph cannot be overstated. The U.S. discipline and composure in the face of adversity was no accident; character starts at the top."

Paper after paper gives prominent play to Brooks's inspirational pregame talk, in which he reminded his team, "You're born to be a player, you're meant to be here." The coach symbolizes the collective ego, the pride of the entire squad.

The coach can symbolize cool, rational authority, "discipline and composure in the face of adversity," but the warmth of personal leadership also emerges. Jim Craig talks about his assistant coach: "And Craig Patrick is our catalyst. To me he's been a father and a brother. His father died less than three weeks ago and he is here. He has made me a man."

While the team has no stars, the individual players emerge clearly in the reporters' vignettes. We read about "scar-faced" Jackie O'Callahan, whose struggle to return from knee surgery has given the team a boost. The key is sacrifice, which gives meaning to the team as well as dramatizing the importance of the entire structure of the Sportsworld. Sacrifice is something Mike Eruzione understands well. His father worked three jobs to help raise six children, and his mother borrowed money to get him started in hockey. "People can relate to us, to what we go through," he says. "We typify the American people. We're striving for a goal. And through hard work we'll achieve it."

The team is a collective unit, but the game is a stage for heroism. In hockey, the goalie is the focal point repelling shots with the dexterity of a contortionist. The goalie's ability to block shots coming at him at speeds approaching 100 miles per hour is the key to the team's success. The goalie is also an inspiration for his teammates. Mike Ramsey points to teammate Craig: "He said before the game, 'I'm only gonna

148

give up two goals.' He sets the standards for himself. He's a helluva goalie."

What makes goalie Craig's heroism even more thrilling is the fact that his courage has been previously questioned. Coach Brooks unceremoniously pulled Craig out of the exhibition game against the Russians at Madison Square Garden. Craig was in danger of being permanently labeled a "choker." Craig's vindication and heroism add to the larger team drama.

The personal lives of the athletes are important vehicles for fan identification. We are treated to inside views of the players and their families; we join their private lives. The much-discussed relationship between Jim Craig and his father epitomizes this process of identification.

The symbolism of the game, the team, and the hero emerges out of Lake Placid into the everyday lives of millions of Americans. *Sports Illustrated* reports a basketball game in Athens, Ohio, being interrupted by the hockey news. In similar fashion, members of a surgical intensive care unit in Miami, Florida, have one eye on the game and another on their patients. New York watering holes were filled with jubilant New Yorkers hugging, cheering, and generally going wild. And, as I attended an important conference on the family held by New York's Governor Hugh Carey, one Hispanic professor of social work, like a child in school at World Series time, had a radio ear plug in his ear in order to follow the action. Cries of "What's the score?" rang out from across the conference room.

The Sportsworld's drama rests on play. One of the key ways of dramatizing the play symbolism is to underscore the youthful innocence of the players. This innocence was further highlighted by the descriptions of the experienced Soviet players, some of whom had played at the Olympic Games in Sapporo, Japan, in 1972. The ecstasy of the American

149

team—again contrasted with the calm Soviet efficiency—taps deeply into the play imagery.

It is crucial to understand the sports drama in order to grasp the personal and political importance of American sports. People begin unconsciously to internalize politically important values through that drama. The drama also enables people to escape—and eventually accept—the harsh realities of political and economic life.

The sports drama is gripping because its representation and symbolic resolution of problems make sense to great numbers of people. The nature of the dramatic setting helps inculcate important values "through the back door."

The "sports creed" is congruent with the "business creed" of the larger society. The sports creed, with its emphasis on hard work, sacrifice, and competitive struggle, has been an important agency for socializing a diverse, multiethnic work force into the world of capitalist production. Creating a productive work force is not an easy task. Workers must be imbued with the acceptance of routine, rigid time calculations and long working hours in cramped conditions. The Sportsworld has been a powerful historical force in developing this spirit. The "blue-collar" nature of the Olympic hockey team underlined this moral infrastructure.

In American society, adhering to the proper values leads to fame and fortune. Those who rise, however, are always reminding us of their humble origins in order to dramatize the openness of the class structure. Our hockey heroes are not the "children of luxury." They have sacrificed in order to triumph. New York *Post* writer Mike Marley emphasizes this point:

150

Their sudden success has not made their helmets swell. And with good reason. They have memories. Dave Silk, the right winger from Boston University, has worked as a house painter and a bouncer in a rock-and-roll joint. Defense-man Jackie O'Callahan grew up across the street from a housing project and tended bar in a campus dive. Burly defense-man Bill Baker sweats summers in a pepper mill alongside his dad.

I have shown that the changes in American society in the last one hundred years have produced similar changes in the Sportsworld. A laissez-faire economic system has evolved into a complex corporate state. The values of rugged individualism were forced to take their place alongside the values of teamwork and smooth cooperation. Individual notions of sacrifice merge with sacrifices for the common good.

The ability of the Sportsworld to adapt its normative structure is further demonstrated by the rising emphasis on consumption. As consumption replaced production as the dominant American ethic, the stars of the Sportsworld emerged as "idols of consumption." The older values of hard work merged with the new money mania. The selling of the Olympians is a case in point: Almost immediately after signing a professional contract, Jim Craig began appearing in a television commercial for Coca-Cola that emphasized and exploited the genuine warmth father and son feel for each other.

The values of sports also merge into a diffuse attachment to "Americanism." The hockey team merely made explicit what is operating on all levels of the American Sportsworld. The fact that the Olympians represented us all—unlike the Dodgers, Yankees, Celtics, Cowboys, etc.—clarified this process of community symbolism. A man in Lake Placid, for example, passed out red-white-and-blue flags. "Go on the street and start waving them," he said. "Tonight we are all proud to be Americans. I got down on my knees this morning and said, 'Dear God, lead our nation to regain its way of life that was established long ago when people gave up their lives for something they believed in.' "

151

The involvement with sports creates a rain-or-shine attachment that dulls the cutting edge of political opposition. As a sister of one of the hockey players said in the tumult after the game, she hadn't seen so many flags since the sixties: "And we were burning them then."

The powerful symbolism of the sports drama overlays the political process itself. Every single newspaper account prominently mentions the phone conversation between President Carter and Coach Brooks, who described the phone call: "He said we had made the American people very proud and reflected the ideals of the country which we stand for."

Notes

1. "PLAY BALL" (pages 1-12)

5 The Sportsworld. Robert Lipsyte, *Sportsworld: An American Dreamland* (New York: Quadrangle, 1976). Lipsyte coined the word Sportsworld and I use it because it captures the way in which sports becomes a vivid alternative reality for sports fans.

6 All their lives. Lipsyte, p. 40.

7 If sports' defenders. Paul Hoch, *Rip Off the Big Game* (New York: Doubleday, 1972). Athletic "alienation" is discussed in Chip Oliver, Ron Rapoport, ed., *High for the Game* (New York: Morrow, 1971), and Dave Meggyesy, *Out of Their League* (Berkeley, California: Ramparts Press, 1970).

9 "Sports is life." Neil Offen, *God Save the Players* (Chicago: Playboy Press, 1974), p. 9.

10 There is a theory. Offen, p. 9.

11 "The world of sports." James Reston, "Sports and Politics in America," *The New York Times* (September 12, 1969).

11 "Sports is a sweaty Oz." *Sportsworld* XI; Ann Leider, "The National Football League and American Life," *The New York Times* (January 18, 1976), Section 5. As Michael Novak has observed in *The Joy of Sports:* "Sports are deeper than politics—deeper than any single political system and deeper in the human heart than political authority. Sports lie at the very root of liberty . . . in the free play of intelligence and imagination . . . (In Heaven, it is rumored, the angels play in the presence of great love and light. Sports yield our metaphors for paradise.) Who imagines that the completely good life would entail *working*, pursuing means towards ends . . . Sports constitutes the place in life where the revolution is already *here*." The point that Novak doesn't make is that the sports utopia is integrated within a larger, much less utopian environment and functions to support that environment (New York: Basic Books, 1976), p. 276.

12 "Sweet closure of anxiety." H. L. Nieburg, *Culture Storm: Politics and the Ritual Order* (New York: St. Martin's Press, 1973).

153

2. "AND THEN I THOUGHT ABOUT THE GAME . . ." (pages 13-33)

15 Last Season. Ray Kennedy and Nancy Williamson, "Money and Sports," *Sports Illustrated* (July 31, 1978); "The Fans: Are They Up in Arms?," *Sports Illustrated* (August 6, 1978), p. 42.

15 "If the Bulldogs." Bill Gilbert, "That Senior Season," *Sports Illustrated* (November 14, 1977), p. 113.

16 The locker room. Bill Russell, *Go Up for Glory* (New York: Coward-McCann, 1966), p. 113.

16 Finally I turned. Frederick Exley, *A Fan's Notes* (New York: Random House, 1968), pp. 15-16.

17 The Republicans. Cited by Larry Merchant in *And Every Day You Take Another Bite* (New York: Dell, 1971), pp. 42-43.

18 Yankee Stadium. Exley, p. 310.

18 "Many artists." Murray Edelman, *The Symbolic Use of Politics* (Champaign, Ill.: University of Illinois Press, 1967), p. 71.

19 Fans, Knick fans especially. Phil Berger, *Miracle on 33rd Street: The New York Knickerbockers Championship Season* (New York: Simon & Schuster, 1970), p. 193.

19 "What schoolyard?" Jay Neugeboren, *Big Man* (New York: Belmont Books, 1970), p. 83.

20 It came quite naturally. See Paul Gallico's wonderfully descriptive and intuitive *Farewell to Sport* (Freeport, New York: Books for Libraries Press, 1970), p. 93.

20 The people yelled. Russell, p. 118.

21 "The hoo-rah." Berger, p. 200.

21 Spectators also help. Orrin Klapp, *The Collective Search for Identity* (New York: Holt, Rinehart & Winston, 1969), p. 191.

21 "But if it all sounds." Russell, p. 128.

21 Walter Mitty adventures. George Plimpton, *Paper Lion* (New York: Pocket Books, 1967); *Out of My League* (New York: Pocket Books, 1967); *Shadow Box* (New York: Putnam, 1977); and "Bozo the Bruin," *Sports Illustrated* (January 28, 1978), pp. 56-64.

21 ". . . the old whack." Plimpton, *Paper Lion*, p. 75.

23 The Knicks took the floor. Berger, p. 251.

23 George Allen. Cited in Studs Terkel's *Working* (New York: Avon , 1972), p. 508.

25 The crowd was at full howl. Arnold Mandell, *The Nightmare Season* (New York: Random House, 1976), p. 146. Another example of this form of victimage is the way in which New York Giant football fans harassed former coach Allie Sherman with "Goodbye, Allie" chants; see Larry Merchant's columns "Ritual Sacrifice I" and "Ritual Sacrifice II" in the *New York Post* (September 17 and 18, 1969).

26 We were running. Russell, pp. 118-119.

26 All the great legends. Gallico, p. 17.

27 "In a time." Hugh Duncan, *Symbols in Society* (New York: Oxford University Press, 1968), p. 131.

27 ". . . if a baseball umpire." Erving Goffman, *The Presentation of the Self in Everyday Life* (New York: Doubleday, 1959), p. 30.

28 The questions of drug use and violence. In chapter fourteen of *The Nightmare Season,* Arnold Mandell discusses Pete Rozelle's star-chamber methods in his investigation of drug abuses on the San Diego Chargers. More recently, NBA Commissioner Larry O'Brien took strong measures against Kermit Washington for breaking an opponent's nose. Most players felt that Washington was being scapegoated to appease an aroused public opinion. See Steve Cady, "Washington Is Reeling from the Punch He Threw," *The New York Times* (December 30, 1977), p. 17.

28 When Mullaney. Berger, p. 254.

29 One of the most. John Wooden, as told to Jack Tobin, *They Call Me Coach* (Waco, Texas: Word Inc., 1973), p. 177. For other examples of racial harmony, see Curt Flood, with Richard Carter, *The Way It Is* (New York: Pocket Books, 1972), chapter four; Roger Kahn, *The Boys of Summer* (New York: New American Library, 1973), p. xv; Bill Bradley, *Life on the Run* (New York: Bantam Books, 1977), p. 140; George Plimpton, *Paper Lion,* p. 168; Jerry Kramer, with Dick Schaap, *Instant Replay* (New York: New American Library, 1969), p. 27; and Jerry Izenberg, *How Many Miles to Camelot? The All-American Sports Myth* (New York: Holt, Rinehart & Winston, 1971), p. 128.

30 The game is. Ron Firmite, "Bowie Stops Charlie's Checks," *Sports Illustrated* (June 28, 1976), p. 22. The courts have traditionally taken a hands-off policy toward both professional and amateur sports, whose ruling bodies are run in a manner similar to a Middle Eastern emirate. Only recently have colleges and athletes been given some judicial protection.

30 "They seemed to be." Milton Gross, "The Knicks Together," *New York Post* (December 8, 1969).

30 I was taking. Russell, p. 56.

31 They were queer. Gallico, p. 7.

32 And is it possible. Kenneth Burke, "The Rhetoric of Hitler's Battle," Stanley Hyman and Barbara Karmiller, eds., *Terms for Order by Kenneth Burke* (Bloomington, Ind.: Indiana University Press, 1964), p. 112.

155

3. "WAIT TILL NEXT YEAR" (pages 34-63)

39 Every contest. Lewis Cole, *A Loose Game: The Sport and Business of Basketball* (Indianapolis, Ind.: Bobbs-Merrill, 1978), p. 174.

41 "The Community *expects.*" Martin Ralbovsky, *Lords of the Lockerroom,* (New York: Peter Wyden, 1974), p. 235.

41 He was not only. John Tunis, *The Kid from Tomkinsville* (New York: Harcourt, Brace & World, 1940), p. 145.

41 A team. John Tunis, *The Keystone Kids* (New York: Harcourt, Brace & World, 1943), p. 23.

42 "The old warrior." Frank DeFord, "I Don't Date Any Women under 48," *Sports Illustrated* (December 5, 1977), p. 36.

42 "Lest he appear." DeFord, "I Don't Date Any Women under 48," p. 52. For other illustrations of this, see Don Kowet, *The Rich Who Own Sports* (New York: Random House, 1977); Dave Anderson, "Roy Boe and the Public Trust," *The New York Times* (May 4, 1978); Sam Goldaper, "Maverick Sonic Owner Gets All the Applause," *The New York Times* (May 24, 1978); Mike Lupica, "Knicks Await Godfather's Move," *Daily News* (October 17, 1978); and Gerald Eskanazai, "Werblin Weighs Changes at the Top," *The New York Times* (May 29, 1978). George Steinbrenner is, of course, the epitome of personally concerned ownership; see Ron Firmite's article, "Yankee Clipper," *Sports Illustrated* (October 10, 1977).

43 I know of a doctor. Offen, p. 10.

43 During a game. Sarah Pileggi, "No End with This End," *Sports Illustrated* (December 12, 1977), p. 33.

44 And Denver loves it. Pileggi, "No End with This End."

44 He could even. John Tunis, *World Series* (New York: Bantam Books, 1969), p. 163.

45 "Discussed avidly." Curry Kirkpatrick, "The Kain-tuck-ee Jubilee," *Sports Illustrated* (December 26-27, 1977), p. 29. See also Dave Kindred, *Basketball: The Dream Game in Kentucky* (Louisville, Ky.: Data Courier, Inc., 1976).

45 In attempting. I have read through more than fifty popular treatments of teams. In addition, I analyzed two straight years of material on teams in *Sports Illustrated* and one year each in *Sport,* the *Basketball Weekly,* and the *Football News.* I also read through the coverage of the entire 1969–1970 championship year of the New York Knickerbockers in the *New York Post* in order to grasp the sense of purpose and drama portrayed in newspaper sports coverage.

46 (Kahn). Kahn, *The Boys of Summer,* p. 108.

46 Writers felt. Berger, p. 191. Dave Kindred's remark in *Basketball: The Dream Game in Kentucky* is apt: "A sportswriter is a basketball player who can type better than he can shoot."

47 "And in the press box." Berger, p. 219. For further illustrations of this point see Bill Bradley's *Life on the Run,* p. 210, where he describes how the Milwaukee papers treated the Knick arrival like an invasion of an enemy army. The *New York Post* tells of Milwaukee's explosive reaction to beating the Knicks (January 3, 1970).

48 It is just. Red Holtzman, with Leonard Lewin, *The Knicks* (New York: Dodd, Mead, 1970), p. 24.

48 If there is. Jeff Greenfield, *The World's Greatest Team: A Portrait of the Boston Celtics, 1957–1969* (New York: Random House, 1976), p. 14.

48 In almost every. See John Underwood's "New Colts Are Mighty Frisky," *Sports Illustrated* (November 17, 1975), for a look at a talented general manager named Joe Thomas; Curry Kirkpatrick, "A Cavalier Attitude Is Paying Off," *Sports Illustrated* (January 12, 1976) for a look at Cleveland coach Bill Fitch; and "Everybody Gets into the Act," *Sports Illustrated* (November 14, 1975) for a look at the way Golden State owner Franklin Mieuli is portrayed as essential for the team's success.

48 The coach must have. "Everybody Gets into the Act" analyzes the importance of the coach's personality in creating team solidarity. The emphasis is that different coaches will have different emotional levels but that success is a result of a congruence between coach and players. This has been aphoristically stated by Al McGuire, who said, "The team should be an extension of a coach's personality. My team is arrogant and obnoxious" (Dave Anderson, *The New York Times,* March 2, 1977). For an explanation of the rise of "personal" ownership, see Ray Kennedy, "Who Are These Guys?," *Sports Illustrated* (January 31, 1977).

49 Lombardi turned. *Instant Replay,* p. 275; Robert Vare, *Buckeye* (New York: Popular Library, 1974); and Jerry Brondfield, *Woody Hayes and the 100-Yard War* (New York: Random House, 1974) point to parallels between Lombardi and Hayes. The term "up" in sports parallels the use of the term "morale" in industrial management.

50 The stories that. Berger, p. 112, and Goffman, chapter two.

50 The lockerroom. Bradley, p. 70, emphasis added.

51 Carey McWilliams. Wilson C. McWilliams, *The Idea of Fraternity in America* (Berkeley: University of California Press, 1973), pp. 1-8. Lionel Tiger, *Men in Groups* (New York: Vintage Books, 1970),

discusses "male bonding" in sports, as does Michael Novak in *The Joy of Sports*.

51 There is much. Bradley, p. 80.

52 "Festival of common delight." George Herbert Mead, *Selected Writings* (Indianapolis, Ind.: Bobbs-Merrill, 1964), p. 296.

52 Greg and I. Kramer, with Schaap, p. 281. See *Life on the Run*, pp. 210-211; these moments are most visibly seen in nonverbal symbolism. The hundreds of photographs of joyous, hugging athletes and the television scenes of jubilation after a big victory are telling. That they resonated deeply with the fans is evidenced by the huge protest-phone calls deluging the CBS switchboard—when the network cut away before the fans could view the Portland Trailblazer locker-room celebration.

52 "Metaphor." Bradley, p. 60.

56 "Sports have supplied." R. Eliot, cited in Harry Edwards's *Sociology of Sport* (Homewood, Ill.: The Dorsey Press, 1974), p. 129. Edwards's research into America's sports creed is a valuable source of information.

57 As he plays. Hugh Duncan, *Communication and Social Order* (New York: Oxford University Press, 1970), p. 78; see also G. H. Mead, *Mind, Self and Society*, Vol. 1 (Chicago: University of Chicago Press, 1934), pp. 152-156.

57 "The artificial time." Reuel Denney, "The Spectatorial Forms," in J. Talamini and C. Page, eds., *Sport and Society: An Anthology* (Boston: Little, Brown, 1973), p. 380.

58 "Baseball is." Novak, p. 59.

58 Mayo. Elton Mayo, *The Social Problems of an Industrial Civilization: Management and the Worker in Alienation and Freedom* (Chicago: University of Chicago Press, 1964), p. 27. This theme is also present—spanning ideological barriers, as Wolin has pointed out—in the work of Wilhelm Reich, *The Mass Psychology of Fascism* (New York: Noonday, 1970). Reich saw politics as an "emotional plague" and searched for solutions to political conflict in sex therapy. This theme is also present in Harold Lasswell's *Psychopathology and Politics* (New York: Viking, 1960). Conflict is to be replaced by the emotional management of a cadre of psychoanalytically trained "administrators."

61 "America had discovered." Foster Rhea Dulles, *America Learns to Play* (New York: Appleton-Century-Crofts, 1965), p. 191.

63 Habermas. Jürgen Habermas, *Toward a Rational Society: Student Protest, Science and Politics,* trans. Jeremy J. Shapiro (Boston: Beacon

Press, 1970), p. 59. Habermas's argument is a creative synthesis of the ideas of the Frankfort School, Max Weber, Sigmund Freud, to mention a few. The argument developed here is similar to Jacques Ellul's in *The Technological Society* (New York: Vintage, 1967).

63 "The public realm." Habermas, p. 104.

4. "IT'S ONLY A GAME" (pages 64-99)

65 If you had. John Mosedale, *The Greatest of All: The 1927 Yankees* (New York: Warner, 1975), p. 20.

69 Dear Abby. "Dear Abby," *New York Post* (June 26, 1979), p. 30. One of the major themes of this chapter is the political importance of understanding everyday life. Important work in this area has been done by Henri Lefebvre, *Everyday Life in the Modern World* (New York: Harper & Row, 1971); Bruce Brown, *Marx, Freud and the Critique of Everyday Life: Toward a Permanent Cultural Revolution* (New York: Monthly Review Press, 1973); Richard Sennett, *The Fall of Public Man; On the Social Psychology of Capitalism* (New York: Random House, 1978); and Christopher Lasch, *The Culture of Narcissism* (New York: Norton, 1979). The work of Erving Goffman is, of course, seminal in this attempt to link social institutions and everyday life.

69 A seemingly apolitical. Gabriel Almond and Sidney Verba, *The Civic Culture* (Boston: Little, Brown, 1965). A careful reading of the literature on political socialization indicates that much politically important learning takes place in seemingly nonpolitical areas. In fact, a great deal of the stability of the American policy rests on apolitical phenomena. See also Dean Jaros, *Socialization to Politics* (New York: Praeger, 1973), p. 19; Robert Lane, *Political Ideology* (New York: The Free Press, 1962), p. 91; and Robert Hess and Judith Torney, *The Development of Political Attitudes in Children* (New York: Irvington Publishers, 1967), p. 34.

70 "There's a love." Cited in Pete Axthelm's *The City Game: Basketball in New York* (New York: Pocket Books, 1971), p. xiii. See also Dave Kindred's *Basketball: The Dream Game in Kentucky* for a description of the same intense devotion in the cities and hamlets of Kentucky. *The American Game,* a recently released film, indicates well how subcultures are linked together through an attachment to basketball.

70 Thus our love. Robert Smith, *Baseball* (New York: Simon & Schuster, 1947), p. 4. As Karl Deutsch has underscored, it is such a symbolic infrastructure that forms the basis for natural communication and political integration. The language and rituals of the

Sportsworld enable citizens from disparate backgrounds to be "available" to one another, while at the same time providing a secure foundation for the development of a personal identity. The historical continuity of baseball in particular and sports in general is a key factor in its role of generating cohesion in the larger society. See Karl Deutsch's *The Nerves of Government: Models of Political Communication and Control* (New York: The Free Press, 1963). Kenneth Keniston in *The Uncommitted: Alienated Youth in American Society* (New York: Dell, 1960) makes a similar point from a social psychological perspective on p. 196.

71 "Because it promises."   Bruno Bettelheim, *The Uses of Enchantment: The Meaning and Importance of Fairy Tales* (New York: Vintage, 1977), p. 137.

71 Political and social institutions.   As Greenstein remarks in *Children and Politics* (New Haven: Yale University Press, 1965, p. 53), "The oft-proclaimed stability of the American political system, in spite of a remarkably heterogeneous population, suggests that powerful psychological mechanisms encouraging political obedience are present."

72 Baseball, too.   Martin Ralbovsky, *Destiny's Darlings* (New York: Hawthorn, 1974).

73 This symbolic separateness.   The work of Johan Huizinga is central to an understanding of play as a symbolic form (the "profoundly aesthetic quality of play"): *Homo Ludens: A Study of the Play Element in Culture* (Boston: Beacon Press, 1955), p. 2. See also Allen Guttman's description of play as "autotelic" in *From Ritual to Record: The Nature of Modern Sports* (New York: Columbia University Press, 1978) and Greg Stone, "The Play of Little Children," in R. E. Herron and Brian Sutton-Smith, eds., *Child's Play* (New York: John Wiley, 1971), which underscores the dramatic and symbolic nature of play. Eugene Frank, "The Oasis of Happiness: Toward an Ontology of Play," in Jacques Ehrmann, ed., *Game, Play, Literature* (Boston: Beacon Press, 1968), stresses the element of human timelessness in "the autonomy of play action," p. 21. For the similarity behind play and games, the work of Sutton-Smith and his collaborators is essential. Games are a more systematic development of the dialect of form and content. Sutton-Smith's criticism of Piaget in "Piaget on Play: A Critique" in *Child's Play* and in Elliott Avedon and Sutton-Smith, *The Study of Games* (New York: John Wiley, 1971), points out how the thinker undervalues the expressive content of games and the centrality of fantasy in mature thinking.

74 In this world.   Howard Senzel, *Baseball and the Cold War* (New York: Harcourt Brace Jovanovich, 1977), p. 140.

74 "To partake." Senzel, p. 145.

75 In those moments. Bradley, p. 221.

75 The sounds were. Cited in Guttman, p. 102.

76 "For many adults." Kenneth Keniston, "Alienation and the Decline of Utopia," in Hendrik M. Ruitenbeek, ed., *Varieties of Modern Social Theory* (New York: Dutton, 1963), p. 88.

76 "The Holden Caulfields." Keniston, p. 87.

76 This I am sure. Robert Smith, p. 7.

76 "What really." Senzel, p. 14, emphasis added.

76 Even out. Senzel, p. 165.

77 Sometimes I'd go out. Ann Byrne Hoffman, ed., *Echoes from the Schoolyard* (New York: Hawthorn, 1977), p. 193.

77 "As a kid." Hoffman, p. 103.

77 One group. Rick Telander, *Heaven Is a Playground* (New York: St. Martin's Press, 1976), p. 261.

78 But first. Ralbovsky, *Destiny's Darlings,* p. 86.

78 The major league park. Robert Smith, p. 256.

79 Everything I know. Hoffman, p. 177.

79 The old Rucker. Axthelm, p. 3.

79 The crowd. Axthelm, p. 5.

80 That may. Robert Smith, p. 3.

80 I was really lucky. Ralbovsky, *Destiny's Darlings,* p. 175.

81 Look, when. Ralbovsky, *Destiny's Darlings,* p. 154.

81 *Small Town.* Arthur Vidich and Joseph Benjamin, *Small Town in Mass Society* (Princeton, N.J.: Princeton University Press, 1958).

81 "They might." Kahn, *The Boys of Summer,* p. 35.

82 "I strode." Kahn, *The Boys of Summer,* p. 34.

82 Benny. Arnold Beisser, *Madness in Sports: Psychosocial Observations on Sports* (New York: Appleton-Century-Crofts, 1967), p. 137. As I will continually emphasize, this is not meant to imply that sports is therapeutic. Benny's symptoms are "managed" but not rooted out. The problem with the critics is that they often will deny that sports even has any cathartic value. It does.

82 "I'm a success." Ralbovsky, *Destiny's Darlings,* p. 107.

82 "Now Mike took." Ralbovsky, *Destiny's Darlings,* p. 191.

83 "I was a real." Meggyesy, p. 11.

83 "And in a pattern." Meggyesy, p. 11.

83 "As far as." Daniel Offer, *The Psychological World of the Teenager* (New York: Basic Books, 1973), p. 42.

84 I watched. Telander, p. 277.

84 I was terrible. Russell, p. 21.

85 I guess I was. Mickey Mantle, *The Quality of Courage: True Stories of Heroism and Bravery* (New York: Bantam Books, 1964), p. 7.

86 "People underestimated." Bradley, p. 75.

86 "I learned." Ralbovsky, *Destiny's Darlings,* p. 156.

86 "If you broke down." Ralbovsky, *Destiny's Darlings,* p. 209.

86 Miracles happen. Mac Davis, *The Greatest in Baseball* (New York: Scholastic Book Services, 1962), p. 77.

87 *"For Olga Kahn."* Roger Kahn, *A Season in the Sun* (New York: Harper & Row, 1977). Kahn has mellowed in his attitude toward his mother's antipathy toward baseball. When he was growing up he used the sport to escape his mother's world, to feel American, and to identify himself more closely with his father, as he explains in *The Boys of Summer.*

87 To sing. Cited by Marc Fasteau in *The Male Machine* (New York: Dell, 1976), p. 111.

87 "Until I got good." David Wolf, *Foul! The Connie Hawkins Story* (Holt, Rinehart & Winston, 1972), p. 4.

87 Connie slept. Wolf, p. 21.

88 "Welcome to Greenfield." *Basketball Special (Sports Quarterly,* 1972–1973), p. 78.

88 Once when asked. Davis, *The Greatest in Baseball,* p. 31.

89 Ralph Garben. Tristram Potter Coffin, *The Illustrated Book of Baseball Folklore* (New York: Seabury Press, 1975), p. 113, emphasis added.

90. "Frank Merriwell." Cited in Robert Boyle, *Sport: Mirror of American Life* (Boston: Little, Brown, 1963).

90 "Simply because." Wiley Umphlett, *The Sporting Myth and the American Experience* (Lewisburg, Pa.: Bucknell University Press, 1975), p. 31.

91 "Of course." Coffin, p. 126.

91 "Can't a guy." Burt L. Standish (pseud.), *Frank Merriwell's Chums* (New York: Street and Smith, 1971), p. 57.

92 "That authentic moral." Senzel, p. 145.

92 I read. Senzel, p. 153.

92 "You know." Tunis, *The Kid from Tomkinsville,* p. 56.

93 "He was one." Tunis, *The Kid from Tomkinsville,* p. 72.

93 Perhaps we can't. Tunis, *The Keystone Kids,* p. 158.

93 You know. John Tunis, *High Pockets* (New York: Harcourt, Brace & World, 1944), p. 170.

93 For now. Tunis, *The Keystone Kids,* p. 198.

94 Different managers. Tunis, *The Kid from Tomkinsville,* p. 183.

94 "Two or three." Tunis, *World Series,* p. 173.

94 "While he sat." Tunis, *The Kid from Tomkinsville,* p. 19.

95 "He felt." Tunis, *The Kid from Tomkinsville,* p. 16.

95 "Unburden his feelings." Clair Bee, *Championship Ball* (New York: Grosset & Dunlap, 1948), p. 20.

95 "All his uncertainty." Bee, *Championship Ball,* p. 22.

95 "He glanced." Bee, *Championship Ball,* p. 22.

96 He is Walt. Walter Jooss, Jr., "The Dawn of the Possible Dream," in *Sports Illustrated* (February 21, 1972), p. 40.

96 "If certain things." Erving, p. 193.

96 "As I grow closer." Senzel, p. 58.

96 "The emotional content." Senzel, p. 65.

97 Roger Angell, *The Summer Game* (New York: Popular Library, 1972), p. 310.

99 Baseball is. Silvia Tennenbaum, "Trying to Love the Yankees," *Newsday* (October 5, 1978), p. 91. For further understanding of the historical dimension, see Joe Gergen, "And America Pauses to Honor Its Past," in *Newsday* (July 21, 1978), p. 78, and Tony Kornheiser, "To Old Fans, Spring Recalls Many Seasons," in *The New York Times* (March 24, 1978).

5. "WHERE HAVE YOU GONE, JOE DIMAGGIO?" (pages 100-128)

102 On the final Sunday. Coffin, p. 151.

102 To a. Mel Allen, with Frank Graham, *It Takes Heart* (New York: MacFadden-Bartell, 1962), p. 15.

103 The pro game. Terkel, *Working,* p. 500.

103 "What deep roars." Robert Smith, p. 234.

104 Then, all of a sudden. Robert Ward, "The Mutilation of a Work of Art," *Sport* (May 1977), p. 108.

104 What makes Monroe. Woody Allen, "A Fan's Notes on Earl Monroe," *Sport* (November 1977), p. 24.

105 "Like a personal friend." Gallico, p. 103.

106 "Who does." Robert Creamer, *Babe: The Legend Comes to Life* (New York: Pocket Books, 1976), p. 245.

107 The perfect shot. Billie Jean King, with Kim Chapin, *Billie Jean* (New York: Harper & Row, 1974), p. 197. The importance of this idea for fans' consciousness is dramatized by the Pro-Keds sneaker ad—"For those moments you feel like a Pro." Here the notion of craftsmanship, joy, and emulation is linked directly to the commodity structure.

107 When I'm in. King, with Chapin, p. 160.

107 "Heroes represent." Umphlett, p. 169.

108 "Baseball had." Dulles, p. 228.

108 "The world seemed." Dulles, p. 228.

108 After the Civil War. Coffin, p. 3.

108 Mark Twain. Quoted in Dulles, p. 141. The energetic involvement of the fans, their overall boisterousness, also contributes to the rising sense of tumult in urban industrial development.

109 As the New England. Robert Smith, p. 7.

110 The ethnic significance. David Reisman and Reuel Denney, "Football in America: A Study in Cultural Diffusion," in David Reisman, ed., *Individualism Reconsidered* (New York: The Free Press, 1954), p. 243. See also Jerry Brondfield, *Rockne* (New York: Random House, 1976).

110 "Yet there was." Robert Smith, p. 99. But even at this time the world is not morally monolithic. The brutally competitive Ty Cobb had many an admirer in the press box and in the stands. See John D. McCallum, *Ty Cobb* (New York: Praeger, 1975).

112 Yet despite. Robert Smith, p. 222.

112 "Never before." Allison Danzig and Peter Brandwein, eds., *Sport's Golden Age* (Freeport, N.Y.: Books for Libraries Press, 1969), p. ix. For a more sophisticated analysis, see Gallico, pp. 100–103.

112 "But nearly." Gallico, p. 15.

112 Ruth incognito. Creamer, p. 12.

114 "Aside from." Creamer, p. 179.

114 No fictional story. Gallico, p. 81.

114 "It is one." Gallico, p. 41.

115 "Mass-produced visions." Stuart Ewen, *Captains of Consciousness: Advertising and the Social Roots of the Consumer Culture* (New York: McGraw-Hill, 1976), p. 45.

115 "Triumph of." Leo Lowenthal, *Literature, Popular Culture, and Society* (Englewood Cliffs, N.J.: Prentice-Hall, 1961), p. 133.

115 Beyond the realm. Ewen, p. 205.

116 He was a unique. Allen, with Graham, p. 58.

116 "Braddock inspired." Allen, with Graham, p. 67. I would be remiss to leave out the symbolic impact that Joe Louis exerted on millions of peer blacks and poor whites. The sharecropper's son generated hope and renewed faith in the American system. See Joe Louis with Edna and Art Rust, *Joe Louis: My Life* (New York: Harcourt Brace Jovanovich, 1978).

117 "No matter how." Tom Dewey, "A Plea for Some Untarnished Athletic Heroes," *The New York Times* (December 25, 1977). See also Frances Mugavaro, "One Vote for Gil Hodges: A Man of Integrity," *The New York Times* (December 25, 1977).

118 The two men. Lipsyte, p. 53. The point should be made that Namath had the real appeal of a rebel. He did do things his own way. His genuineness was the foundation for his Xeroxed heirs. See particularly Barry McDermott's "Back to Bruce in a Moment, First, This Commercial" in *Sports Illustrated* (September 26, 1977) for an understanding of the growth of contrivance through a look at the packaging of Bruce Jenner.

118 Namath drove. Merchant, p. 166.

119 "Gerulaitis." Nick Seitz, "The Playboy Plays Tough Tennis," *Sport* (September 1977). Gerulaitis, we are told, also owns a $45,000 Rolls-Royce. For further illustrations of this trend, see Bob Wischinia, "Faultless Frank," *Sport* (December 1977); Wilt Chamberlain and Gary Shaw, *Wilt* (New York: Macmillan, 1973); and Ron Firmite, "Reggie, Reggie, Reggie," *Sports Illustrated* (October 1977).

119 Namath, Fleming, Huey. Joe Namath with Dick Schaap, *I Can't Wait Until Tomorrow . . . 'Cause I Get Better Looking Every Day* (New York: New American Library, 1970), p. 69. On page 75 Namath tells us, "I drink for the same reason I keep company with girls. It makes me feel good. It takes away the tension." See also Mary Fleming, "Women Made My Career," *Sport* (May 1977), and Linda Huey, "I Gravitate toward Jocks," *Sport* (May 1977). See also Neil Offen's discussion of "Detroit Shirley," in *God Save the Players!*, Grace Lichtenstein's "There's Something about a Man in Uniform," *Esquire* (October 1974); and Dan Wakefield's "My Love Affair with Billie Jean King," *Esquire* (October 1974). For a revealing description

of an orgy, see chapter nine of Arnold Mandell's *The Nightmare Season*.

119   Tommy John.   John Radosta, "Courageous Comeback Pitcher," *The New York Times* (November 23, 1978). For similar themes about Ron Guidry, see Phil Pepe, "He Dropped Out of a Tree House," *Daily News* (June 20, 1978), and Murray Chase, "Ron Guidry: Breezing Along at the Top," *The New York Times* (March 4, 1979).

120   Larry Bird.   Mark Engel, "Now, a Word about Mr. Bird," *The Basketball Weekly* (January 12, 1978).

121   Pete Rose.   Dick Young, "Clean Living and Dirty Uniforms Pay Off," *Daily News* (December 6, 1978). See also Dave Anderson, "The Little Boy in the Rose Deal," *The New York Times* (December 7, 1978), and Henry Hecht, "Charlie Hustles Off to Philly," *New York Post* (December 6, 1978). Two typical examples of Dick Young's vitriol are "Even on Sinking Ships, Showboats Perform," *Daily News* (December 28, 1977), and "Nets Give King Something to Sit On: The Bench," *The Boston Globe* (January 1, 1978).

121   Vince Papali.   Curry Kirkpatrick, "Very Short and Sweet in Atlanta," *Sports Illustrated* (November 14, 1977); Paul Bellow, "For Lou Piccone the Suicide Squad Is a Living," *Sport* (April 1977); and Robert Jones, "Recovering from a Rocky Start," *Sports Illustrated* (October 3, 1977).

121   "A tough period."   Bob Ward, "Suddenly It's Over, The NBA Odyssey of Jim Barnett," *Sport* (March 1977), p. 59.

122   "I've been preparing."   Bradley, p. 189.

122   "I loved it."   Bradley, p. 189.

122   I cheered.   Exley, p. 134.

123   Margaret Mead.   Quoted in David Potter, *People of Plenty: Economic Abundance and the American Character* (Chicago: University of Chicago Press, 1954), p. 54.

123   Karen Horney.   Karen Horney, *The Neurotic Personality of Our Time* (New York: Norton, 1937), and *Neurosis and Human Growth* (New York: Norton, 1950). My reliance here on Horney's analysis should not be taken as an acceptance of her "revision" of Freud nor as an acceptance of her distinction between the "neurotic" and the "normal." For further insights on these themes, see Rollo May, *The Meaning of Anxiety* (New York: Norton, 1977), and Maurice Stein, Arthur Vidich, and David Manning White, eds., *Identity and Anxiety: The Survival of the Person in Mass Society* (New York: The Free Press, 1960).

124   The "killer instinct."   Bob Cousy, with John Deugney, *The Killer*

Instinct (New York: Random House, 1974), p. 4. As Horney remarks on page 284 of *The Neurotic Personality of Our Time*, "Modern culture is economically based on the principle of individual competition. The isolated individual has to fight with other individuals of the same group to surpass them and frequently to thrust them aside."

125 The most popular thing. Gallico, pp. 17-18.

125 If we could. Gallico, p. 17. This can be exemplified by an exchange between Oakland "assassin" George Atkinson and a young fan: " 'You gonna play the Steelers again soon?' 'I hope so,' George said . . . 'Me, too,' the kid said. 'Then you can get that crybaby Lynn Swann again. Oh, I loved the way you took him out. That was some hit . . . Oooh . . . was that great' " (Robert Ward, "The Oakland Raiders' Charming Assassin," *Sport*, April 7, 1977, p. 53). Much hatred is channeled into the scapegoating of ritual victims—coaches and players alike. See Arnold Mandell's *The Nightmare Season* and Ray Fitzgerald's article on Sidney Wicks, "Sidney, You've Arrived," *The Boston Globe* (January 1, 1978), p. 26.

127 Harvey Kellerman. Cited in Offen, pp. 206–207.

127 In a moment. Exley, p. 237. Daniel Boorstin remarks, "We risk being the first people in history to make their illusions so vivid, so persuasive, so 'realistic,' that we can live in them" (*The Image*, New York: Atheneum, 1962, p. 240).

128 "The dialectical relation." Franz Neumann, "Anxiety and Politics," in Stein, Vidich, and White. As Marshall Berman remarks, "Thus the freedom or repression, equality or inequality in a state is a function, not of its merely political organization but of the structure of its personal and social life as a whole" (*The Politics of Authenticity: Radical Individualism and the Emergence of Modern Society*, New York: Atheneum, 1970, p. 7).

6. OF TEAM PLAYERS AND SKY HOOKS (pages 129-142)

132 "One measure." Red Smith, "Spoken Like a True Son of Old Whittier," *The New York Times* (April 30, 1973). See also James Reston, "Sports and Politics in America," *The New York Times* (September 12, 1969). The emphasis on language here is designed to show how symbolism is transmitted or conveyed through language.

135 Failing to. Meg Greenfield, "Get on the Raft with Taft, Boys," *Newsweek* (June 7, 1976).

135 "Politics is." David Reisman, with Nathan Glazer and Reuel Denney, *The Lonely Crowd: A Study of the Changing American Character* (New Haven: Yale University Press, 1953), p. 189. See also Lasch, chapter three.

136 "The world of sports." Reston, "Sports and Politics in America."

136 Everyone needs. Beisser, p. 129.

137 With the rise. John Betts, *America's Sporting Heritage* (Reading, Mass.: Addison-Wesley, 1974).

137 "It was Patterson." Jerome Holtzman, *No Cheering in the Press Box* (New York: Holt, Rinehart & Winston, 1973), p. 23.

137 "Informality of style." Perry Tannenbaum and James Noah, "Sportugese: A Study in Sports Page Communication," in John Loy and Gerald Kenyon, *Sport, Culture, and Society* (New York: Macmillan, 1969).

137 "It is clear." Tannenbaum and Noah, p. 336. See also *Sportsworld*, p. 122. As Erwin Canham of *The Christian Science Monitor* once said, "News must be made more interesting and compelling which means *simplification* and *dramatization* are imperative. The result is that the news is sometimes 'souped-up' to the language of the sports page which finds its way into events that are too grave to be considered in such terms" (Stanley Woodward, *The Sports Page,* New York: Greenwood Press, 1968, p. 420).

138 "I believed in it." Jerome Holtzman, p. 72. The preponderance of writers interviewed by Holtzman expressed a similar view. Stanley Woodward in *The Sports Page* feels that sportswriting more and more resembles the rest of the paper. My observation is that this is not necessarily true unless we take the incongruous position that the rise of sports language in the rest of the paper is bringing *it* closer to the sports page rather than the other way around. See Tannenbaum and Noah, "Sportugese," p. 327, for a similar view.

138 "Spectatorship involves." C. H. Page, "Reaction to Stone Preservation," in *Aspects of Contemporary Sports Sociology,* G. S. Kenyon, ed. (Chicago: The Athletic Institute, 1969), quoted by Barry McPherson, "Sports Consumption and the Economics of Consumerism," in D. Ball and John Loy, eds., *Sport and the Social Order* (Reading, Mass.: Addison-Wesley, 1975).

138 According to. This is illustrated as well in "Sportugese," where Tannenbaum and Noah note a high communication coefficiency between sportswriters and sports fans. The kinds of verbs that the writer uses indicate to the fan the nature of the final point spread between teams. "However, for the person who does not read or follow sports, these verbs fail in communicating their message" (Woodward, p. 424).

139 "Football was always." Gary Wills, *Nixon Agonistes: The Crisis of the Self-Made Man* (Boston: Houghton Mifflin, 1970), p. 161.

139 "Team" metaphor.   William Safire, *Safire's Political Dictionary: The New Language of Politics* (New York: Random House, 1978), page 633. Mr. Safire was extremely helpful in the preparation of this chapter.

139 It became fashionable.   Wills, p. 162. See also James David Barber, *Presidential Character* (Englewood Cliffs, N.J.: Prentice-Hall, 1972), pp. 388-393.

Bibliography

The Sportsworld Library

Allen, Maury. *Where Have You Gone, Joe DiMaggio? The Story of America's Last Hero.* New York: New American Library, 1975.

Allen, Mel, with Frank Graham. *It Takes Heart.* New York: MacFadden-Bartell, 1962.

Angell, Roger. *Five Seasons: A Baseball Companion.* New York: Simon & Schuster, 1977.

————. *The Summer Game.* New York: Popular Library, 1972.

Asinoff, Eliot. *Eight Men Out: The Black Sox and the 1919 World Series.* New York: Holt, Rinehart & Winston, 1963.

Axthelm, Pete. *The City Game: Basketball in New York.* New York: Pocket Books, 1971.

Ball, D., and Loy, John (eds.). *Sport and Social Orders.* Reading, Mass.: Addison-Wesley, 1975.

Bannister, Roger. *The Four-Minute Mile.* New York: Dodd, Mead, 1957.

Bee, Clair. *Championship Ball.* New York: Grosset & Dunlap, 1948.

————. *Touchdown Pass.* New York: Grosset & Dunlap, 1947.

Beisser, Arnold. *Madness in Sports: Psychosocial Observations on Sports.* New York: Appleton-Century-Crofts, 1967.

Berger, Phil. *Miracle on 33rd Street: The New York Knickerbockers Championship Season.* New York: Simon & Schuster, 1970.

Betts, John. *America's Sporting Heritage.* Reading, Mass.: Addison-Wesley, 1974.

Bouton, Jim. *Ball Four.* New York: World, 1970.

————. *I'm Glad You Didn't Take It Personally.* New York: Dell, 1971.

Boyle, Robert. *Sport: Mirror of American Life.* Boston: Little, Brown, 1963.

Bradley, Bill. *Life on the Run.* New York: Bantam Books, 1977.

Brady, John, and Hall, James (eds.). *Sports Literature.* New York: McGraw-Hill, 1975.

Brondfield, Jerry. *Rockne.* New York: Random House, 1976.

————. *Woody Hayes and the 100-Yard War.* New York: Random House, 1974.

Brosnan, Jim. *The Long Season.* New York: Harper & Row, 1960.

Brunner, Bernard. *Six Days to Sunday.* New York: Ballantine Books, 1975.

Cannon, Jack, and Cannon, Tom (eds.). *Nobody Asked Me, But . . . The World of Jimmy Cannon*. New York: Holt, Rinehart & Winston, 1978.

Chamberlain, Wilt, and Shaw, Gary. *Wilt: Just Like Any Other 7-Foot Black Millionaire Who Lives Next Door*. New York: Macmillan, 1973.

Chapin, Dwight, and Prugh, Jeffrey. *The Wizard of Westwood: Coach John Wooden and His UCLA Brains*. Boston: Houghton Mifflin, 1973.

Chapin, Henry (ed.). *Sports in Literature*. New York: David McKay, 1976.

Christopher, Matt. *Lucky Seven Sports Stories*. Boston: Little, Brown, 1970.

———. *That Basket Counts*. Boston: Little, Brown, 1971.

Clark, Tom. *The World of Damon Runyon*. New York: Harper & Row, 1978.

Coffin, Tristram Potter. *The Illustrated Book of Baseball Folklore*. New York: Seabury Press, 1975.

Cohen, Marvin. *Baseball the Beautiful: Decoding the Diamond*. New York: Links Books, 1974.

Cohen, Stanley. *The Game They Played*. New York: Farrar, Straus & Giroux, 1977.

Cole, Lewis. *A Loose Game: The Sport and Business of Basketball*. Indianapolis, Ind.: Bobbs-Merrill, 1978.

Coover, Robert. *The Universal Baseball Association, Inc., J. Henry Waugh, Prop*. New York: Random House, 1968.

Cosell, Howard. *Cosell*. New York: Pocket Books, 1973.

Cousy, Bob, with John Deugney. *The Killer Instinct*. New York: Random House, 1974.

Creamer, Robert. *Babe: The Legend Comes to Life*. New York: Pocket Books, 1976.

Danzig, Allison, and Brandwein, Peter (eds.). *Sport's Golden Age*. Freeport, N.Y.: Books for Libraries Press, 1969.

Davis, Mac. *Basketball's Unforgettables*. New York: Bantam Books, 1972.

———. *The Greatest in Baseball*. New York: Scholastic Book Services, 1962.

DeBusschere, Dave, with Paul Zimmerman and Dick Schaap (eds.). *The Open Man: A Championship Diary*. New York: Grove Press, 1970.

DeFord, Frank. *Big Bill Tilden: The Triumphs and the Tragedy*. New York: Simon & Schuster, 1976.

Delillo, Don. *End Zone*. Boston: Houghton Mifflin, 1972.

Denlinger, Kenny Loy, and Shapiro, Leonard. *Athletes for Sale*. New York: Thomas Y. Crowell, 1975.

Devaney, John. *Bart Starr*. New York: Scholastic Book Services, 1967.

Dickey, Glenn. *The Jock Empire: Its Rise and Deserved Fall.* Radnor, Pa.: Chilton, 1974.

Dulles, Foster Rhea. *America Learns to Play.* New York: Appleton-Century-Crofts, 1965.

Durocher, Leo, with Ed Linn. *Nice Guys Finish Last.* New York: Pocket Books, 1976.

Durso, Joseph. *The Sports Factory: An Investigation into College Sports.* New York: Quadrangle, 1975.

Edwards, Harry. *The Revolt of the Black Athlete.* New York: The Free Press, 1969.

———. *The Sociology of Sport.* Homewood, Ill.: The Dorsey Press, 1973.

Exley, Frederick. *A Fan's Notes.* New York: Random House, 1968.

Fitzgerald, Ray. *That Championship Feeling: The Story of the Boston Celtics.* New York: Scribner's, 1975.

Flood, Curt, with Richard Carter. *The Way It Is.* New York: Pocket Books, 1972.

Gallico, Paul. *Farewell to Sport.* Freeport, N.Y.: Books for Libraries Press, 1970.

Gehrig, Eleanor, and Durso, Joseph. *My Luke and I.* New York: New American Library, 1976.

Gemme, Leila. *The New Breed of Athlete.* New York: Washington Square Press, 1975.

Gilmartin, Joe. *The Little Team That Could . . . The Fabulous Rise of the Phoenix Suns.* Phoenix, Ariz.: The Phoenix Suns, 1976.

Gipe, George. *The Great American Sports Book.* New York: Doubleday, 1978.

Gold, Robert (ed.). *The Roar of the Sneakers.* New York: Bantam Books, 1977.

Golenback, Peter. *Dynasty: The New York Yankees, 1949–1964.* Englewood Cliffs, N.J.: Prentice-Hall, 1975.

Greenfield, Jeff. *The World's Greatest Team: A Portrait of the Boston Celtics, 1957–1969.* New York: Random House, 1976.

Guttman, Allen. *From Ritual to Record: The Nature of Modern Sports.* New York: Columbia University Press, 1978.

Hart, M. Marie. *Sport in the Socio-Cultural Process.* Dubuque, Iowa: Wm. C. Brown, 1972.

Hoch, Paul. *Rip Off the Big Game: The Exploitation of Sports by the Power Elite.* N.Y.: Doubleday, 1972.

Hoffman, Ann Byrne (ed.). *Echoes from the Schoolyard.* New York: Hawthorn, 1977.

Holtzman, Jerome. *No Cheering in the Press Box*. New York: Holt, Rinehart & Winston, 1973.

Holtzman, Red, with Leonard Lewin. *The Knicks*. New York: Dodd, Mead, 1970.

Honig, Donald. *Baseball Between the Lines*. New York: Coward, McCann & Geoghegan, 1976.

———. *Baseball When the Grass Was Real*. New York: Coward, McCann & Geoghegan, 1975.

Ibrahim, Hilm. *Sport and Society*. Los Alamitos, Calif.: Hwong Publishing Co., 1976.

Isaacs, Neil. *Jock Culture, USA*. New York: Norton, 1978.

Izenberg, Jerry. *How Many Miles to Camelot? The All-American Sports Myth*. New York: Holt, Rinehart & Winston, 1971.

Jackson, Phil, with Charles Rosen. *Maverick: More Than a Game*. Chicago: Playboy Press, 1975.

Jenkins, Dan. *Semi-Tough*. New York: New American Library, 1972.

Jordon, Pat. *The Suitors of Spring*. New York: Dodd, Mead, 1970.

Kahn, Roger. *The Boys of Summer*. New York: New American Library, 1973.

———. *A Season in the Sun*. New York: Harper & Row, 1977.

Kaufman, Louis; Fitzgerald, Barbara: and Sewell, Tom. *Moe Berg: Athlete, Scholar . . . Spy*. Boston: Little, Brown, 1974.

Kenyon, Gerald (ed.). *Aspects of Contemporary Sports Sociology*. Chicago, Ill.: The Athletic Institute, 1970.

Kindred, Dave. *Basketball: The Dream Game in Kentucky*. Louisville, Ky.: Data Courier, Inc., 1976.

King, Billie Jean, with Kim Chapin. *Billie Jean*. New York: Harper & Row, 1974.

Kolatch, Jonathan. *Sports, Politics and Ideology in China*. New York: Jonathan David, 1972.

Koppett, Leonard. *The New York Times at the Super Bowl*. New York: Quadrangle, 1974.

Kowet, Don. *The Rich Who Own Sports*. New York: Random House, 1977.

Kramer, Jerry. *Lombardi: Winning Is the Only Thing*. New York: Pocket Books, 1970.

Kramer, Jerry, with Dick Schaap (ed.). *Instant Replay*. New York: New American Library, 1969.

Larner, Jeremy. *Drive, He Said*. New York: Bantam Books, 1970.

Layman, Richard, and Bruccoli, Matthew (eds.). *Some Champions, Sketches and Fiction by Ring Lardner*. New York: Scribner's, 1976.

Leib, Fred. *Baseball As I Have Known It*. New York: Grosset & Dunlap, 1977.

Leonard, George. *The Ultimate Athlete: Revisioning Sports, Physical Education and the Body*. New York: Viking, 1974.

Libby, Bill. *The Coaches*. Chicago: Henry Regnery, 1972.

Lipsyte, Robert. *Sportsworld: An American Dreamland*. New York: Quadrangle, 1976.

Lorimer, Lawrence (ed.). *Breaking In: Nine First-Person Accounts about Becoming an Athlete*. New York: Dell, 1974.

Louis, Joe, with Edna and Art Rust. *Joe Louis: My Life*. New York: Harcourt Brace Jovanovich, 1978.

Lowe, Ben; Kanin, David; and Strenk, Andrew (eds.). *Sport and International Relations*. Champaign, Ill.: Stipes Publishing Company, 1978.

Loy, John, and Kenyon, Gerald (eds.). *Sport, Culture, and Society*. New York: Macmillan, 1969.

Malamud, Bernard. *The Natural*. New York: Dell, 1971.

Mandell, Arnold. *The Nightmare Season*. New York: Random House, 1976.

Mandell, Richard. *The Nazi Olympics*. New York: Macmillan, 1971.

Mantle, Mickey. *The Quality of Courage: True Stories of Heroism and Bravery*. New York: Bantam Books, 1964.

McCallum, John D. *Ty Cobb*. New York: Praeger, 1975.

McCormick, Wilfred. *The Right-End Option*. New York: Grosset & Dunlap, 1965.

———. *The Three-Two Pitch*. New York: Grosset & Dunlap, 1966.

McPhee, John. *A Sense of Where You Are: A Profile of William Warren Bradley*. New York: Farrar, Straus & Giroux, 1965.

Mead, William. *Even the Browns: The Zany, True Story of Baseball in the Early Forties*. Chicago: Contemporary Books, 1978.

Meggyesy, Dave. *Out of Their League*. Berkeley, Calif.: Ramparts Press, 1970.

Merchant, Larry. *And Every Day You Take Another Bite*. New York: Dell, 1971.

Michener, James. *Sports in America*. New York: Random House, 1976.

Mitchell, Jerry. *The Amazing Mets*. New York: Grosset & Dunlap, 1964.

Morton, Henry. *Soviet Sport*. New York: Collier Books, 1963.

Mosedale, John. *The Greatest of All: The 1927 Yankees*. New York: Warner, 1975.

Murphy, Michael. *Golf in the Kingdom*. New York: Dell, 1972.

Namath, Joe, with Bob Oates. *A Matter of Style*. Boston: Little, Brown, 1973.

Namath, Joe, with Dick Schaap. *I Can't Wait Until Tomorrow . . . 'Cause I Get Better Looking Every Day*. New York: New American Library, 1970.

Neugeboren, Jay. *Big Man*. New York: Belmont Books, 1970.

Noll, Roger (ed.). *Government and the Sports Business*. Washington, D.C.: The Brookings Institution. 1974.

Novak, Michael. *The Joy of Sports*. New York: Basic Books, 1976.

Offen, Neil. *God Save the Players*. Chicago: Playboy Press, 1974.

Oliver, Chip, with Ron Rapoport. (ed.). *High for the Game*. New York: Morrow, 1971.

Olsen, Jack. *Alphabet Jackson*. New York: Bantam Books, 1975.

———. *The Black Athlete: A Shameful Story*. New York: Time-Life Books, 1969.

———. *Massey's Game*. Chicago: Playboy Press, 1976.

Orr, Jack (ed.). *Baseball's Greatest Players*. New York: J. Lowell Pratt, 1963.

Parr, Jeanne. *The Super Wives: Life with the Giant Jocks*. New York: Coward, McCann & Geoghegan, 1976.

Parrish, Bernie. *They Call It a Game*. New York: New American Library, 1972.

Parrott, Harold. *The Lords of Baseball*. New York: Praeger, 1976.

Paul, William Henry. *The Gray-Flannel Pigskins: Movers and Shakers of Pro Football*. Philadelphia: Lippincott, 1974.

Pepe, Phil. *Kareem Abdul-Jabbar*. New York: Grosset & Dunlap, 1973.

Peterson, Robert. *Only the Ball Was White*. Englewood Cliffs, N.J.: Prentice-Hall, 1970.

Plimpton, George. *Mad Ducks and Bears*. New York: Random House, 1973.

———. *Out of My League*. New York: Pocket Books, 1967.

———. *Paper Lion*. New York: Pocket Books, 1967.

———. *Shadow Box*. New York: Putnam, 1977.

Ralbovsky, Martin. *Destiny's Darlings: A World Championship Little League Team Twenty Years Later*. New York: Hawthorn, 1974.

———. *Lords of the Lockerroom*. New York: Peter Wyden, 1974.

———. *The Namath Effect*. Englewood Cliffs, N.J.: Prentice-Hall, 1976.

Rentzel, Lance. *When All the Laughter Died in Sorrow*. New York: Saturday Review Press, 1972.

Rice, Damon. *Seasons Past.* New York: Praeger, 1976.

Rice, Grantland. *The Tumult & the Shouting.* New York: Barnes, 1954.

Ritter, Lawrence. *The Glory of Their Times: The Story of the Early Days of Baseball Told by the Men Who Played It.* New York: Collier Books, 1966.

Roberts, Michael. *Fans! How We Go Crazy Over Sports.* Washington, D.C.: The New Republic Book Company, 1976.

Robinson, Brooks, with Fred Bauer. *Putting It All Together.* New York: Hawthorn, 1971.

Rooney, John. *A Geography of American Sport: From Cabin Creek to Anaheim.* Reading, Mass.: Addison-Wesley, 1974.

Rosen, Charles. *Scandals of '51: How the Gamblers Almost Killed College Basketball.* New York: Holt, Rinehart & Winston, 1978.

Russell, Bill. *Go Up for Glory.* New York: Coward-McCann, 1966.

Sage, George (ed.). *Sport and American Society.* Reading, Mass.: Addison-Wesley, 1970.

Sahadi, Lou. *The Long Pass: The Spectacular Inside Story of Joe Namath and the N.Y. Jets.* New York: Bantam Books, 1969.

Sample, Johnny, with Fred J. Hamilton and Sonny Schwartz. *Confessions of a Dirty Ballplayer.* New York: Dell, 1971.

Schaap, Dick. *Quarterbacks Have All the Fun.* Chicago: Playboy Press, 1974.

Schecter, Leonard. *The Jocks.* Indianapolis, Ind.: Bobbs-Merrill, 1969.

Schoor, Gene. *Football's Greatest Coach: Vince Lombardi.* New York: Pocket Books, 1975.

Scott, Jack. *The Athletic Revolution.* New York: The Free Press, 1971.

———. *Bill Walton: On the Road with the Portland Trail Blazers.* New York: Thomas Y. Crowell, 1976.

Senzel, Howard. *Baseball and the Cold War.* New York: Harcourt Brace Jovanovich, 1977.

Shaw, Gary. *Meat on the Hoof.* New York: St. Martin's Press, 1973.

Shula, Don, with Lou Sahadi. *The Winning Edge.* New York: Dutton, 1973.

Smith, Leverett. *The American Dream and the National Game.* Bowling Green, Ohio: Bowling Green University Popular Press, 1975.

Smith, Red. *Strawberries in the Wintertime: The Sporting World of Red Smith.* New York: Quadrangle, 1974.

Smith, Robert. *Baseball.* New York: Simon & Schuster, 1947.

Solomon, George. *The Team that Nobody Wanted: The Washington Redskins.* Chicago: Henry Regnery, 1973.

Standish, Burt (pseud.). *Frank Merriwell's Chums*. New York: Street and Smith, 1971.

———. *Frank Merriwell's Schooldays*. New York: Street and Smith, 1971.

Sugar, Bert Randolph. *Hit the Sign and Win a Free Suit of Clothes from Henry Finkelstein*. Chicago: Contemporary Books, 1978.

Sullivan, George. *Bart Starr: The Cool Quarterback*. New York: Putnam, 1973.

———. *Wilt Chamberlain*. New York: Grosset & Dunlap, 1966.

Talamini, John, and Page, Charles (eds.). *Sport and Society: An Anthology*. Boston: Little, Brown, 1973.

Telander, Rick. *Heaven Is a Playground*. New York: St. Martin's Press, 1976.

———. *Joe Namath and the Other Guys*. New York: Holt, Rinehart & Winston, 1976.

Tuite, James (ed.). *The Arthur Daley Years*. New York: Quadrangle, 1975.

Tunis, John. *All American*. New York: Harcourt, Brace and World, 1945.

———. *High Pockets*. New York: Harcourt, Brace and World, 1944.

———. *Iron Duke*. New York: Harcourt, Brace and World, 1946.

———. *The Keystone Kids*. New York: Harcourt, Brace and World, 1943.

———. *The Kid from Tomkinsville*. New York: Harcourt, Brace and World, 1940.

——— *Sports, Heroes and Hysterics*. New York: John Day, 1928.

———. *World Series*. New York: Bantam Books, 1969.

Tutko, Thomas, and Burns, William. *Winning Is Everything and Other American Myths*. New York: Macmillan, 1976.

Umphlett, Wiley. *The Sporting Myth and the American Experience*. Lewisburg, Pa.: Bucknell University Press, 1975.

Vare, Robert. *Buckeye: A Study of Coach Woody Hayes and the Ohio State Football Machine*. New York: Popular Library, 1974.

Voight, David Q. *America through Baseball*. Chicago: Nelson-Hall, 1976.

Weiss, Paul. *Sport: A Philosophic Inquiry*. Carbondale, Ill.: Southern Illinois University Press, 1969.

West, Jerry, with Bill Libby. *Mr. Clutch: The Jerry West Story*. New York: Grosset & Dunlap, 1969.

Wolf, David. *Foul! The Connie Hawkins Story*. New York: Holt, Rinehart & Winston, 1972.

Wooden, John, as told to Jack Tobin. *They Call Me Coach*. Waco, Texas: Word Books, 1973.

Woodward, Stanley. *The Sports Page*. New York: Greenwood Press, 1968.

Woolf, Robert. *Behind Closed Doors*. New York: New American Library, 1976.

Yablonsky, Louis, and Brower, Jonathan. *The Little League Game: How Kids, Coaches and Parents Really Play It*. New York: Quadrangle, 1979.

The View from Beyond the Arena

Almond, Gabriel, and Verba, Sidney. *The Civic Culture: Political Attitudes and Democracy in Five Nations*. Boston: Little, Brown, 1965.

Avedon, Elliott, and Sutton-Smith, Brian. *The Study of Games*. New York: John Wiley, 1971.

Barber, James David. *Presidential Character*. Englewood Cliffs, N.J.: Prentice-Hall, 1972.

Berman, Marshall. *The Politics of Authenticity, Radical Individualism and the Emergence of Modern Society*. New York: Atheneum, 1970.

Bettelheim, Bruno. *The Uses of Enchantment: The Meaning and Importance of Fairy Tales*. New York: Vintage, 1977.

Brown, Bruce. *Marx, Freud and the Critique of Everyday Life: Toward a Permanent Cultural Revolution*. New York: Monthly Review Press, 1973.

Deutsch, Karl. *The Nerves of Government: Models of Political Communication and Control*. New York: The Free Press, 1963.

Duncan, Hugh. *Communication and Social Order*. New York: Oxford University Press, 1970.

———. *Symbols in Society*. New York: Oxford University Press, 1968.

Edelman, Murray. *The Symbolic Uses of Politics*. Champaign, Ill.: University of Illinois Press, 1967.

Ehrmann, Jacques, ed. *Game, Play, Literature*. Boston: Beacon Press, 1968.

Ellul, Jacques. *The Technological Society*. New York: Vintage, 1967.

Ewen, Stuart. *Captains of Consciousness: Advertising and the Social Roots of the Consumer Culture*. New York: McGraw-Hill, 1976.

Fasteau, Marc. *The Male Machine*. New York: Dell, 1976.

Goffman, Erving. *The Presentation of the Self in Everyday Life*. New York: Doubleday, 1959.

Greenstein, Fred. *Children and Politics*. New Haven: Yale University Press, 1965.

Habermas, Jürgen. *Toward a Rational Society: Student Protest, Science and Politics*. Translated by Jeremy J. Shapiro. Boston: Beacon Press, 1970.

Herron, Robin, and Sutton-Smith, Brian (eds.). *Child's Play*. New York: John Wiley, 1971.

178

Hess, Robert, and Torney, Judith. *The Development of Political Attitudes in Children*. New York: Irvington Publishers, 1967.

Horney, Karen. *Neurosis and Human Growth*. New York: Norton, 1950.

————. *The Neurotic Personality of Our Time*. New York: Norton, 1937.

Huizinga, Johan. *Homo Ludens: A Study of the Play Element in Culture*. Boston: Beacon Press, 1955.

Hyman, Stanley, and Karmiller, Barbara (eds.). *Terms for Order by Kenneth Burke*. Bloomington, Ind.: Indiana University Press, 1964.

Jaros, Dean. *Socialization to Politics*. New York: Praeger, 1973.

Keniston, Kenneth. *The Uncommitted: Alienated Youth in American Society*. New York: Dell, 1960.

Klapp, Orrin. *The Collective Search for Identity*. New York: Holt, Rinehart & Winston, 1969.

Lane, Robert. *Political Ideology*. New York: The Free Press, 1962.

Lasch, Christopher. *The Culture of Narcissism*. New York: Norton, 1979.

Lasswell, Harold. *Psychopathology and Politics*. New York: Viking, 1960.

Lasswell, Harold, and Associates. *Language of Politics: Studies in Quantitative Semantics*. Cambridge, Mass.: MIT Press, 1965.

Lefebvre, Henri. *Everyday Life in the Modern World*. New York: Harper & Row, 1971.

Lowenthal, Leo. *Literature, Popular Culture, and Society*. Englewood Cliffs, N.J.: Prentice-Hall, 1961.

McWilliams, Wilson C. *The Idea of Fraternity in America*. Berkeley, Calif.: University of California Press, 1973.

May, Rollo. *The Meaning of Anxiety*. New York: Norton, 1977.

Mayo, Elton. *The Social Problems of an Industrial Civilization: Management and the Worker in Alienation and Freedom*. Chicago: University of Chicago Press, 1964.

Mead, George Herbert. *Mind, Self and Society*. Vol. 1. Chicago: University of Chicago Press, 1934.

————. *Selected Writings*. Indianapolis, Ind.: Bobbs-Merrill, 1964.

Nieburg, H. L. *Culture Storm: Politics and the Ritual Order*. New York: St. Martin's Press, 1973.

Offer, Daniel. *The Psychological World of the Teenager*. New York: Basic Books, 1973.

Potter, David. *People of Plenty: Economic Abundance and the American Character*. Chicago: University of Chicago Press, 1954.

Reich, Wilhelm. *The Mass Psychology of Fascism.* New York: Noonday, 1970.

Reisman, David, ed. *Individualism Reconsidered.* New York: The Free Press, 1954.

Reisman, David; Glazer, Nathan; and Denney, Reuel. *The Lonely Crowd: A Study of the Changing American Character.* New Haven: Yale University Press, 1953.

Ruitenbeek, Hendrik M. (ed.). *Varieties of Modern Social Theory.* New York: Dutton, 1963.

Safire, William. *Safire's Political Dictionary: The New Language of Politics.* New York: Random House, 1978.

Sennett, Richard. *The Fall of Public Man: On the Social Psychology of Capitalism.* New York: Random House, 1978.

Stein, Maurice; Vidich, Arthur; and White, David Manning (eds.). *Identity and Anxiety: The Survival of the Person in Mass Society.* New York: The Free Press, 1960.

Terkel, Studs. *Working.* New York: Avon, 1970.

Tiger, Lionel. *Men in Groups.* New York: Vintage, 1970.

Vidich, Arthur, and Benjamin, Joseph. *Small Town in Mass Society.* Princeton, N.J.: Princeton University Press, 1958.

Wills, Gary. *Nixon Agonistes: The Crisis of the Self-Made Man.* Boston: Houghton Mifflin, 1970.

Index

C